THE FANTASTIC WORL
OPTICA
ILLUSIONS

I dedicate this collection to Elizabeth and Laura Seckel.

Published by Firefly Books Ltd., 2002

U.S. Publisher Cataloging-in-Publication Data
Seckel, A.
Great book of optical illusions / A. Seckel.–1st ed.
304 p. ; col. ill. ; photos. : cm.
Summary : Selection of over 280 optical illusions from historical and modern sources.
ISBN 1-55297-650-5 (pbk.)

1. Optical illusions. I. Title.
152.14/ 8 21   CIP   QP495.S44 2001

National Library of Canada Cataloguing in Publication
Seckel, Al
Great book of optical illusions / Al Seckel.
ISBN 1-55297-650-5
1. Optical illusions. I. Title.
QP495.S42 2002   152.14'8   C2002-901526-X
ISBN: 1-55297-650-5

First published in Canada in 2002 by
Firefly Books Ltd.
3680 Victoria Park Avenue
Toronto, Ontario M2H 3K1

First published in the United States in 2002 by
Firefly Books (U.S.) Inc.
P.O. Box 1338, Ellicott Station
Buffalo, New York 14205

Project Editor: Vanessa Daubney
Project Art Direction: Jim Lockwood
Production: Lisa French

Printed and bound in Dubai

ILLUSIONWORKS
The World's Premier Optical Illusion Art Brand

IllusionWorks, L.L.C. is the World's Premier Optical Illusion Art Brand. Please visit our award-winning website (www.illusionworks.com), which features all sorts of dynamic and interactive illusions, illusory artwork, and in-depth scientific explanations.

For information on the illusion on page 1 please see page 272.
Opposite: Modified Hermann Grid: What happens when you move your eyes across this picture? In this modification of the classic Hermann Grid illusion, the intersection points are colored white rather than the yellow of the classic Hermann grid. This leads to the occurrence of a new color effect. Around the spot on which the eye is fixed, the intersections remain white. Away from this point they flash lilac; as the eye scans the picture, the colored areas move, too. When the distance from which the picture is viewed is increased, their number multiplies.

ILLUSION WORKS

THE GREAT BOOK OF
OPTICAL
ILLUSIONS

Al Seckel

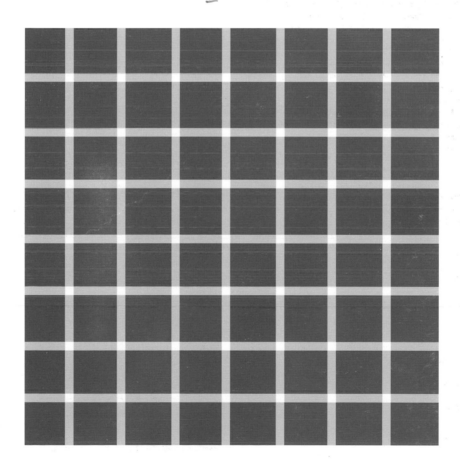

FIREFLY BOOKS

CONTENTS

INTRODUCTION

Many books on optical illusions reprint the same examples over and over again, but this is not the case in the Great Book of Optical Illusions. I have deliberately selected examples that are not familiar so that the reader has a much greater chance of being surprised. You will find innumerable illusions that are not found in any other published source, making this volume by far the most comprehensive collection of illusions ever published.

Many of these illusions come from recent work in vision and perception laboratories, and others come from a variety of modern artists who have deliberately incorporated an "obvious" illusion into a drawing, photograph, or sculpture. There were also quite a number of illusions that were created specially by us. Of course, you will find the familiar classics here too, making this volume an invaluable reference tool for those interested in studying illusions.

The illusions are not ordered in any systematic fashion, but are grouped into galleries. At the back of each section you will find some notes that provide brief scientific explanations of our (and, in some cases, my own) best guesses for why these effects occur, and how they are consistent with the processes that mediate normal perception. The reader will also find that the explanations will become more comprehensive in the second half of the book. I expand on the underlying explanations as the reader becomes more familiar with the workings of the perceptual system. At the end of the book is a glossary of technical terms that are used throughout the text as well as suggestions for further reading. Although the book is in a popular format and accessible to all ages, it can serve as a stepping stone to some wonderful projects on perception for students of all ages.

Most of us take vision for granted. We seem to do it so effortlessly; however, perceiving images, objects, and motion is a very complicated process. Only in the last one hundred years, and especially in the last twenty years, have scientists started to make some progress in understanding vision and perception.

How we "sort it out" is a truly wonderful process; however, this process mainly happens in our brain and not in our eyes! Light waves come into our eyes and then enter photoreceptive cells on our retinae. These retinal images, whether from a two-dimensional image or from our three-dimensional world, become semi-flat representations on a curved surface. Because of this, there is an inherent ambiguity in the retinal output to the brain. For any given retinal image, there are an infinite variety of possible inputs that could give rise to the same output. Your visual system, however, usually settles for the correct interpretation. That is what the brain does – it interprets, and it needs to do it fast! There are some very powerful hidden constraints on just how your brain does this, but those same constraints can also cause illusions. Vision scientists study illusions, because illusions are a wonderful window into perception.

They can reveal the hidden constraints of our perceptual system in a way that normal vision can not.

You do not see many illusions in the real world because your visual system has evolved so many ways to resolve the inherent ambiguity in a retinal image. Visual perception is essentially an ambiguity solving process. Sometimes, an illusion occurs when there is not enough information in the image to resolve the ambiguity. For example, important clues that would normally be present, and which would have resolved the ambiguity, are missing. Other illusions take place because an image violates a constraint based on an underlying regularity of our world. In other cases, illusions occur because two or more different constraints are in conflict. This means that your visual system can interpret the scene in more than one way. Even though the image on your retina remains constant, you never see an odd mixture of the two perceptions, although the two interpretations may perceptually flip back and forth. Many other illusions in this book are intentionally created objects or scenes that have "accidental" alignments, where the true shape of the object perceived is cleverly obscured and controlled from a fixed viewpoint. Nature is normally not so devious, and so your visual system assumes that you perceive objects from a "generic point of view," unless there is evidence to the contrary.

Part of the fun of this book will involve being tricked, fooled, and misled. This collection of illusions will definitely do that! It has nothing to do with how smart you are, how cultured you are, how artistic you are, or how old you are. You will be tricked. In fact, many of the illusions are so powerful you will doubt the written description, while others are so convincing that you will perceive nothing wrong. This means you must read the caption that accompanies each image! Only then will you get the full impact of this volume.

Vision Science is one of the most exciting areas in modern research, and the study of illusions is one that brings great joy. It needs to be emphasized, though, that our understanding of vision and perception is very far from complete and the explanations provided in this volume are tentative and should be regarded with some degree of skepticism, especially since some of the explanations involve my own speculations! I really hope that this collection will inspire some serious thought – and practical demonstrations – as to why these effects occur. It is my sincere hope that this may lead to some new insights about the creative intelligence of vision as well as bringing delight to both young and old alike, as it stimulates thought and discussion about the most marvelous mystery in the universe – the human brain. Now, go have some fun!

Al Seckel
California Institute of Technology, 2002

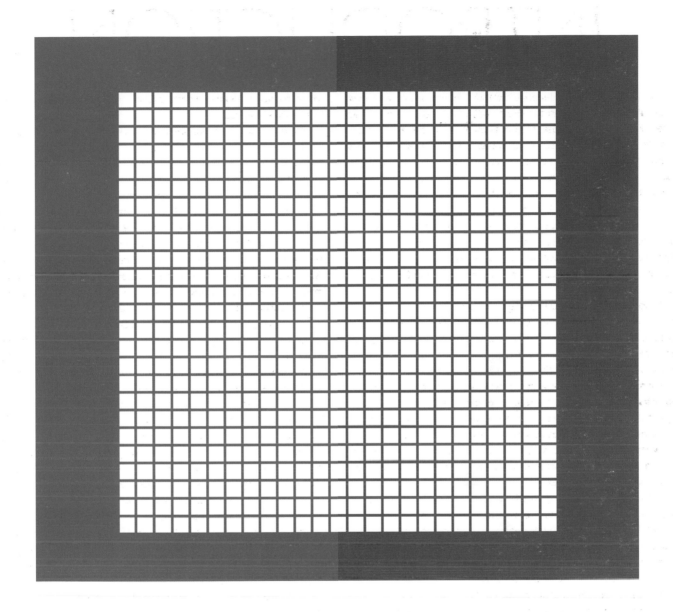

Color Assimilation: Do you perceive a reddish hue within the white squares on the right and a bluish hue within the white squares on the left? See page 302.

GALLERY

I

1 **Shepard's Tabletop:** These two tabletops are absolutely identical in size and shape! If you don't believe it, trace only the tabletops and see for yourself.

Previous page: **Fraser's Spiral** is one of the most powerful illusions known. What you see appears to be a spiral, but it is really a series of perfect concentric circles! This illusion is so powerful that it has been known to induce incorrect finger tracing!

2 **Extent and Perspective:** Although they appear to be dramatically different in length, lines AB and CD are equal.

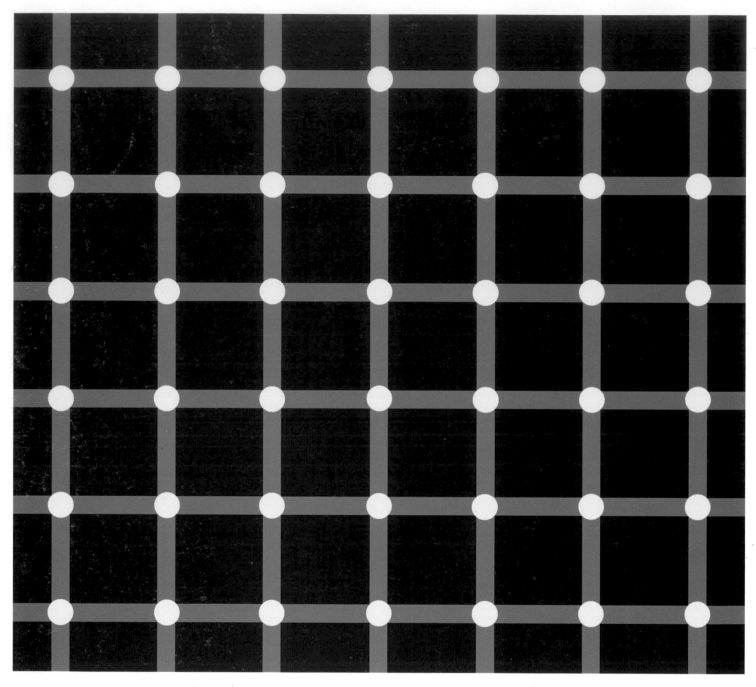

3 **The Scintillating Grid:** The disks at the junctions will appear to flash when you move your eyes around this image.

4 **Checker Shadow:** The light check inside the shadow is identical to the dark check outside the shadow. If you don't believe it, cut out a peephole exactly the size of each square and test it!

5 **Escher's Impossible Box**. Belgian artist Matheau Haemakers, drawing his inspiration from a print by the Dutch graphic artist M.C. Escher, has created a physical model of an impossible box.

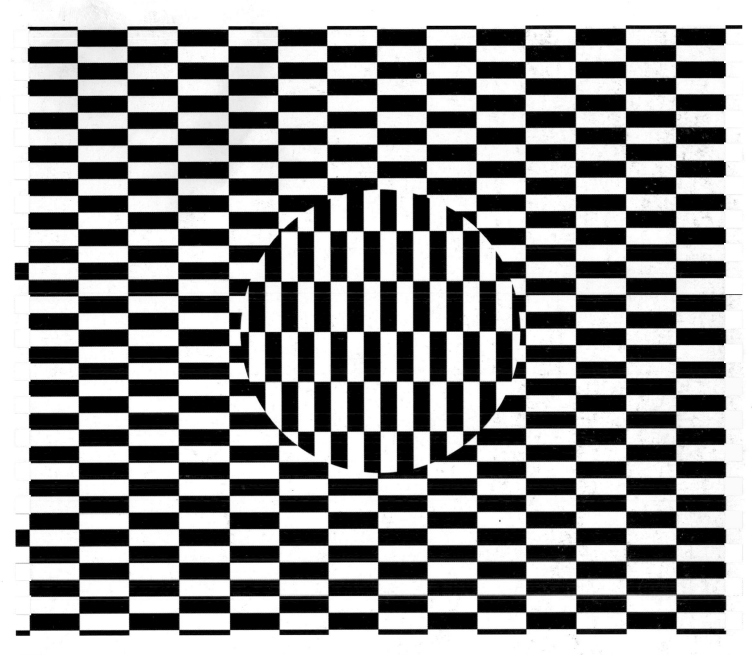

6 **Ouchi Illusion:** Move the page back and forth. The center section may appear to move in a direction different from its surroundings. The center section will also appear to be at a different depth.

7 **Man on the Moon:** This image of Buzz Aldrin's helmet was made out of a collage of space images.

9 **Crazy Nuts:** Can you figure out how the straight steel rod miraculously passes through the seemingly perpendicular holes?

10 **Figure/Ground:** What is hiding here? Before you check out the answer, search carefully, because once you perceive the hidden image, you will never be able to see this image in its meaningless state again.

11 **Kissing Couple Illusion:** An illusory kiss by American artist Jerry Downs.

12 **Impossible Staircase:** What happens
when you walk around this peculiar
staircase? Where is the bottom or top step
located?

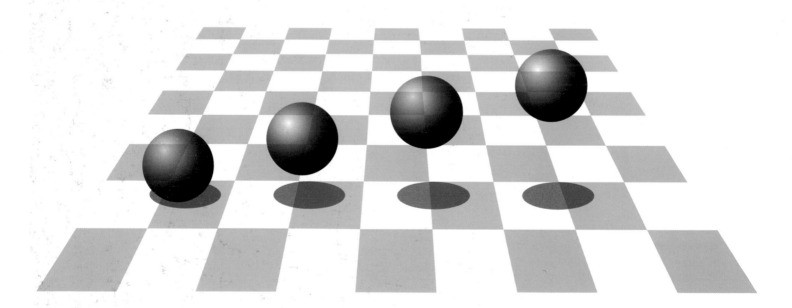

13 **Ball and Shadow Illusion:** Are the balls in the two illustrations in different positions relative to the background?

14 **Vanity:** Is there danger lurking for this couple?

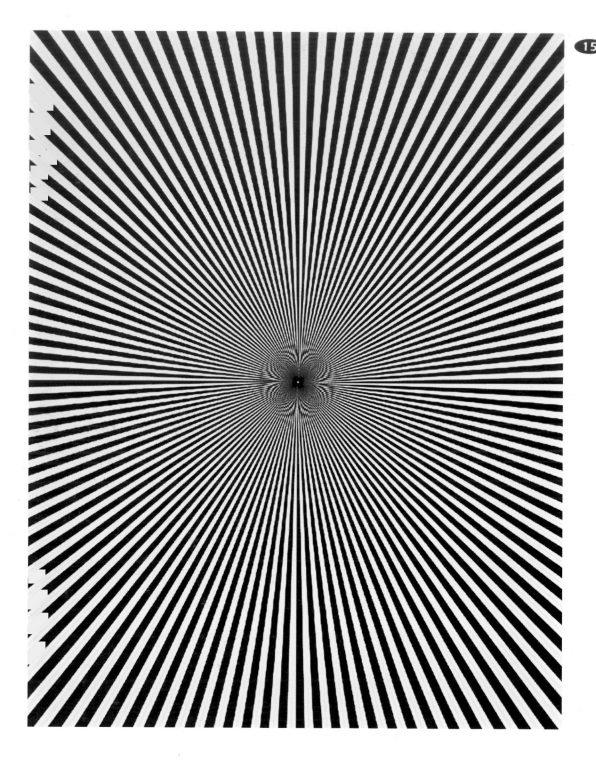

15 **Shimmer:** Move the page and you will perceive a shimmering swirl around the center. The colors are yellow and black, but you may see other colors as well.

16 **The Hallway Illusion:** Is the small man standing in the foreground the same size as the man standing in the background?

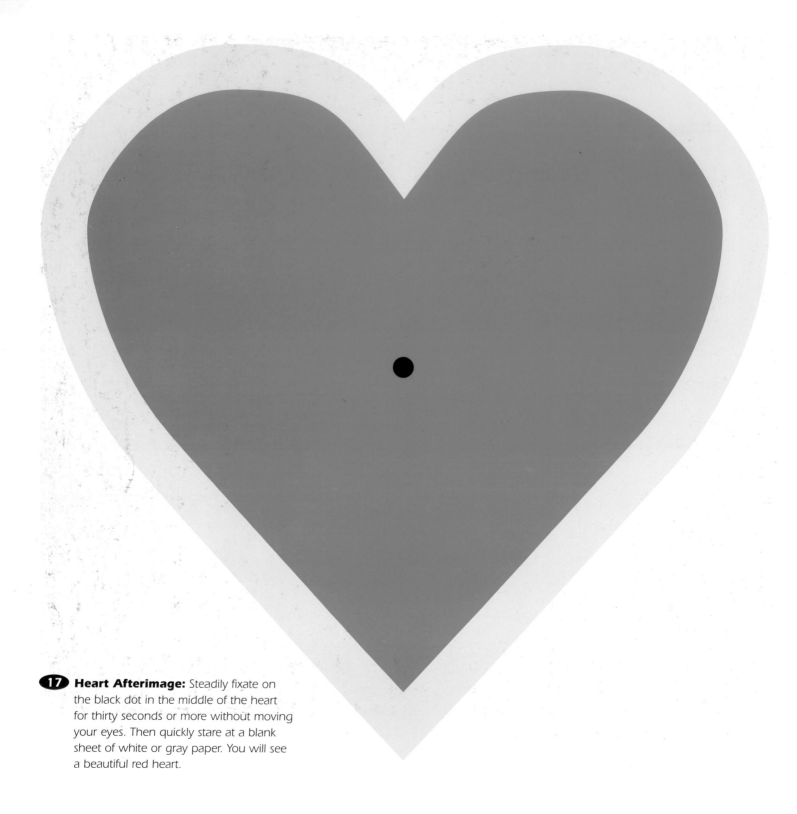

17 **Heart Afterimage:** Steadily fixate on the black dot in the middle of the heart for thirty seconds or more without moving your eyes. Then quickly stare at a blank sheet of white or gray paper. You will see a beautiful red heart.

18 **Poggendorf Illusion:** What colored line is co-linear with the white line?

19 **"The Mysterious Lips that Appeared on the Back of my Nurse.":** The great Spanish surrealist painter Salvador Dalí entitled this work, "The Mysterious Lips that Appeared on the Back of my Nurse."

20 **Continuous Line Illusion:** These squares may look perfect and separated, but they are formed by one continuous line.

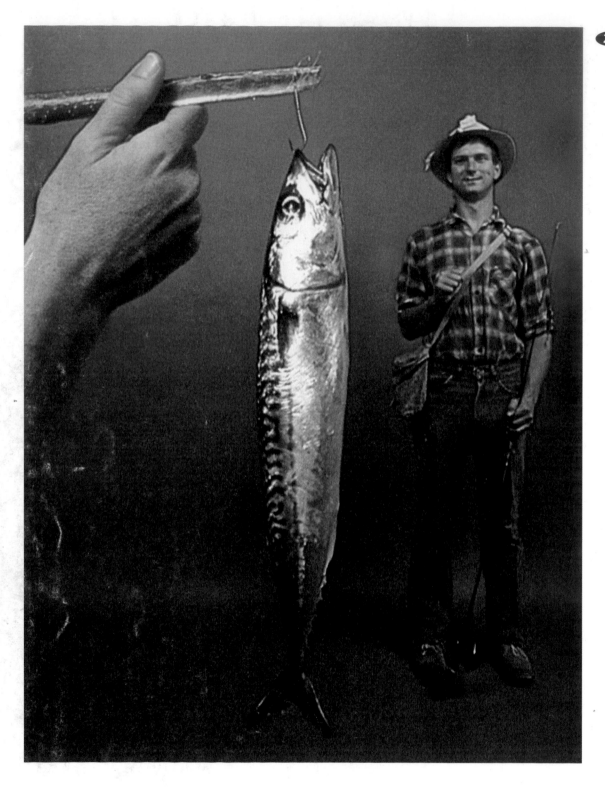

21 **Context Size Illusion:** Cover the man and the fish appears to be a normal size. Cover the hand and the fish is a rather remarkable catch.

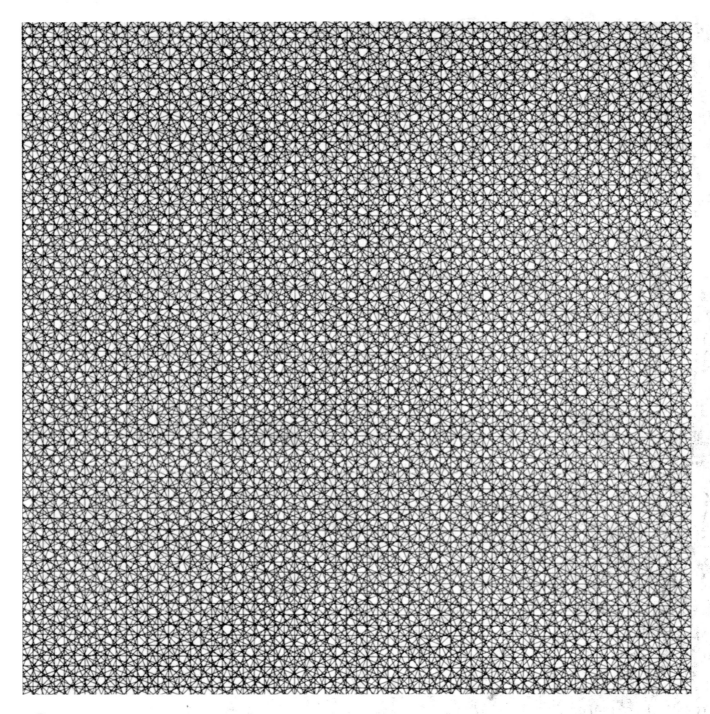

22 **Morellet's Tirets Illusion:** Move your eyes around this image and small circles will appear to scintillate and fade.

23 **Reutersvärd's Impossible Triangle:**
Here is an interesting version of the
impossible triangle by Swedish artist Oscar
Reutersvärd.

24 **Color Depth Illusion:** Stare at this figure for a while and the green area will appear to separate in depth. Tilting the page and viewing the image from above seems to help facilitate viewing this illusion.

25 **Aristotle's Illusion:** Aristotle's illusion is a most peculiar tactile illusion. Try crossing the first and second fingers of one hand. If the nose is rubbed gently with the inner surfaces of the crossed fingers – which are normally their outer edges – one may experience two noses!

26 **Ambiguous Horse Illusion:** Which way is the horse facing? Jerry Downs created this photo illusion.

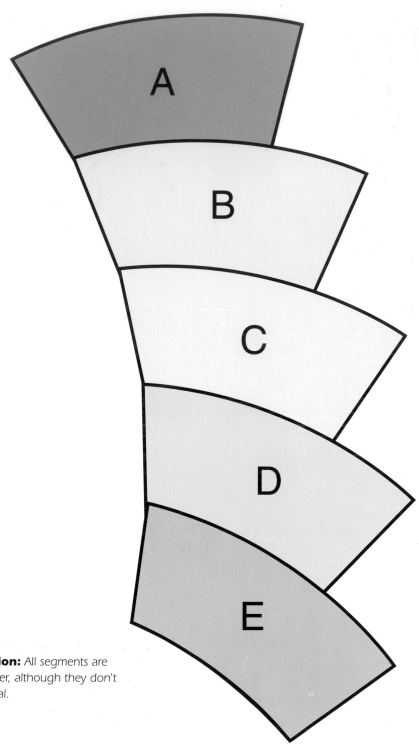

27 **Wundt Area Illusion:** All segments are identical to each other, although they don't appear to be identical.

1000
20
30
1000
1030
1000
+   20
_____

? ? ? ?

28 **Priming Illusion:** This is a wonderful priming illusion involving simple addition that will fool bank tellers and mathematicians. Add up the row of numbers out loud in groups. What is your answer? Do it again. Most people get the wrong answer! Try it on your friends for hilarious results. Only look at the correct answer after you have tried it.

29 **Stereo Line Illusion:** Hold the illustration so that it is just below both eyes and that the image lies flat and perpendicular to your face. Look at the two lines with both eyes and after a while a third line will appear to rise out of the page.

30 **Twisted Cord Illusion:** The vertical lines appear to bend, although they are all perfectly straight and parallel to each other.

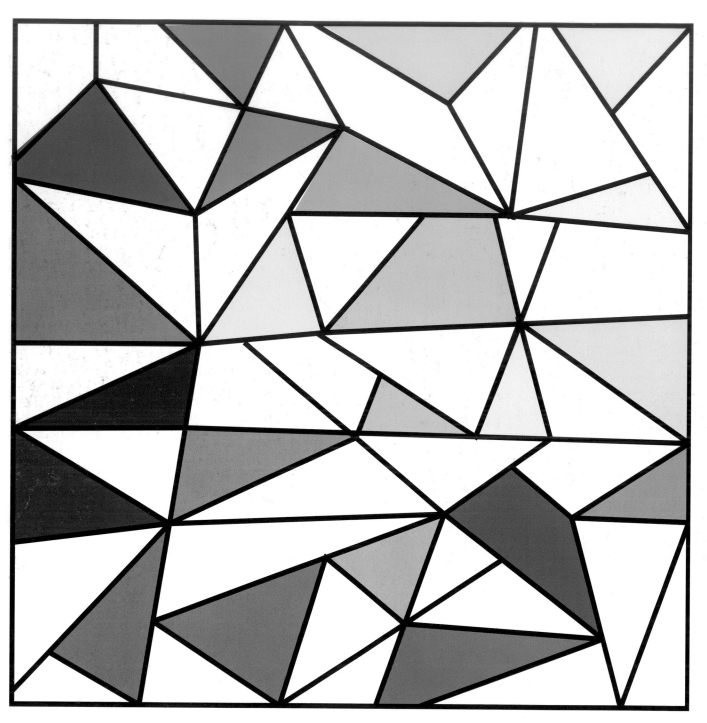

32 **Find the Hidden Star:** Can you find the five-pointed star hidden in the pattern. Search carefully before you seek the answer.

33 This is not a Magritte:
This photographer caught an unusual painting by an artist.

34 **Floating Finger Illusion:** You can make a finger float right before your eyes in this fun illusion. Hold your two hands in front of your face at eye level. Keep the tips of your index fingers also at eye level. Focus on a wall several feet behind your fingers. You should see a finger float. Try moving your fingers closer to your face. What happens? If you focus on your fingers, instead of the wall, the illusion vanishes.

35 **Physical Model of an Impossible Triangle:** This triangle is possible in the mirror, but impossible as seen outside the mirror. How can that be?

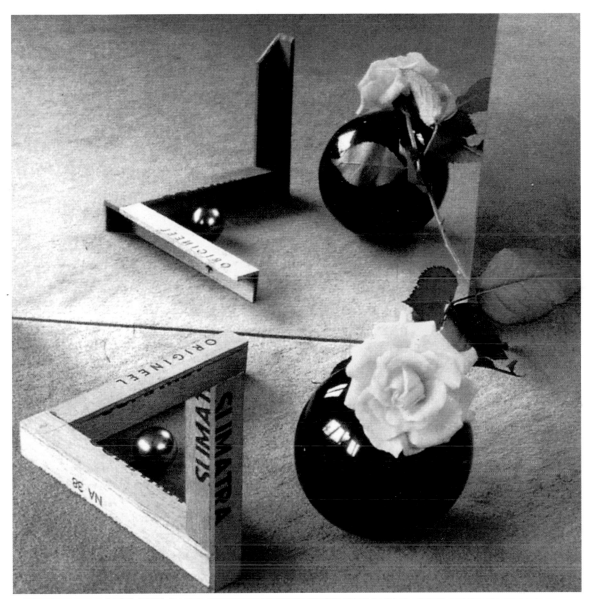

Notes on Gallery I

Fraser's Spiral (Page 9)
The perceived "twist" at each portion of the circle is transmitted across the entire circle to produce the spiral effect. Cover half of the illustration and the illusion will no longer work. English psychologist James Fraser created a whole series of these twisted cord illusions in 1906.

1. Shepard's Tabletop
Although the drawing is flat, it suggests a three-dimensional object. The table's edges and legs provide perspective cues that influence your interpretation of its three-dimensional shape and constancy. This powerful illusion clearly demonstrates that your brain does not take a literal interpretation of what it sees. Stanford psychologist Roger Shepard created this tabletop illusion.

2. Extent and Perspective
Again, perspective cues provide a three-dimensional context for perceiving length.

3. The Scintillating Grid
German vision scientists Michael Schrauf and E. R. Wist discovered the Scintillating Grid illusion in 1997. It is not yet fully understood what causes this effect.

4. Checker Shadow
The light check does not look dark because your visual system interprets the darkness as belonging to the shadow and not to the check. MIT vision scientist Ted Adelson recently designed this incredible brightness illusion.

6. Ouchi Illusion
The intersections between the vertical texture and the horizontal texture seem to trigger your visual system's motion detectors in different ways. When the page is moved back and forth you will perceive illusory motion in depth. It was discovered in 1977 by the Japanese op-artist Hajime Ouchi.

9. Crazy Nuts
The nuts are actually hollow, but appear to be convex, so the holes are not perpendicular to each other. The Crazy Nuts have been lit from below (normally light comes from above), which gives incorrect information about their true three-dimensional shape. American magician Jerry Andrus created this wonderful illusion.

10. Figure/Ground
It is a Dalmatian dog. Once you perceive the dog, the picture becomes dramatically reorganized with certain parts of the dots being grouped with the dog and others with the background. This illustrates the importance of prior experience on visual perception, especially if the organization and meaning of the image is highly ambiguous. Once your visual system ascribes meaning to a particular image, the meaningful interpretation dominates. This is also an example of a non-reversible figure/ground illusion.

12. Impossible Staircase
There is no bottom or top staircase. That is why it is impossible. The impossible staircase, first created by geneticist Lionel Penrose in the mid 1950s, served as inspiration for M. C. Escher's classic print, "Ascending and Descending."

13. Ball and Shadow Illusion
In the top illustration, the balls appear to be resting on the surface and receding into the distance. In the bottom illustration, the balls appear to be rising above the surface and not receding. The only difference between the two illustrations is the placement of the cast shadows, which provide a context for interpreting the three-dimensional position of the ball relative to the background. Without a shadow the position of the balls is ambiguous. Vision scientists Dan Kersten and David Knill first described this effect in 1996.

14. Vanity
The meaning of this image will flip-flop between a skull and a couple sitting at a table. This 1920s French postcard featuring a skull or two lovers became a popular motif throughout the 20th century inspiring such artists as Salvador Dalí.

15. Shimmer
It is not fully understood what causes this illusion.

16. Hallway Illusion
The very small man standing in the bottom right of the passageway is the same man from the background who has been digitally copied to the foreground. There is no difference in size, except that he is placed further away from the horizon. Perspective information also gives the strong impression of depth in a receding corridor. As an object recedes into the distance against a perspective background, not only does its visual angle become smaller, but it also moves closer to the visual horizon. This illusion is similar in some ways to the Ponzo illusion.

17. Heart Afterimage
The color receptors in your eye actually work in pairs: red/green and blue/yellow. When the red receptors become fatigued the green receptor will dominate and vice versa. This is known as a color afterimage.

18. Poggendorf Illusion
The yellow line is co-linear with the white line. This is a powerful variant of the classic 19th century Poggendorf illusion. There are many theories about why this simple geometrical illusion occurs, but none proposed to date gives a satisfactory account for all the conditions under which it diminishes or appears. It could be that your visual system is extremely poor at interpreting the path of diagonal lines, although it not understood why.

20. Continuous Line Illusion
Although this illusion is not well understood, we do know that your visual system is extremely poor at curve-tracing. Your eye cannot determine the relative placement of fine lines without tracing them, and even then performs very poorly.

21. Context Size Illusion
What you perceive sometimes is dependent upon context. Irvin Rock developed this context size illusion.

22. Morellet's Tirets Illusion
Your visual system tends to prefer organization and groups, so it searches for the "best" interpretation. In most images there is a way to group and organize the image. However, in this painting "Tirets" by French artist Francois Morellet, there is no "best" interpretation. Rather, there are lots of possible circles. As you scan this image, your visual system is constantly searching for the "best" interpretation; however, many continuously arise.

24. Color Depth Illusion
Canadian vision researcher Jocelyn Faubert discovered this new color depth illusion.

25. Aristotle's Illusion
You are used to feeling the left side of an object with your left finger and the right side of an object with your right finger. When you cross your fingers your motor system and your tactile system give conflicting information about what is where, sometimes resulting in the experience of a second nose.

27. Wundt Area Illusion
Although this classic illusion was discovered over 100 years ago, it is still not fully understood.

28. Priming Illusion
The correct answer is 4100.

29. Stereo Line Illusion
This particular viewpoint causes the image in each eye to fuse together; resulting in a third line that appears in stereo.

30. Twisted Cord Illusion
This illusion happens early on in the visual system, when your retinae encode edges and contours. It is known as a twisted cord illusion.

31. Poggendorf Illusion with Pillars
There is nothing wrong with the arches. This illusion is a variation on the classic Poggendorf illusion.

32. Find the Hidden Star
Look in the bottom right region. The puzzle is difficult because there are too many possible ways to group the lines. However, once the star has been pointed out, you will never be able to see it in its meaningless state again. The great American master of puzzles Sam Lloyd created this classic figure/ground puzzle.

34. Floating Finger Illusion
By focusing on the wall, the two fingers in the foreground incorrectly overlap when the images from both eyes are automatically combined. These overlapping images produce a stereogram with the floating finger.

35. Physical Model of an Impossible Triangle
This physical model of an impossible triangle only works from only one special angle. Its true construction is revealed in the mirror. Even when presented with the correct construction of the triangle (as seen in the mirror), your brain will not reject its seemingly impossible construction (seen outside the mirror). This illustrates that there is a split between your conception of something and your perception of something. Your conception is ok, but your perception is fooled.

36. Shape from Shading
Your brain uses clues to determine depth in a 2D picture. One clue is the shading. Normally, light comes from above. By turning the figure around, your brain receives clues that light is coming from another angle, and thus the same shading will correspond to another shape.

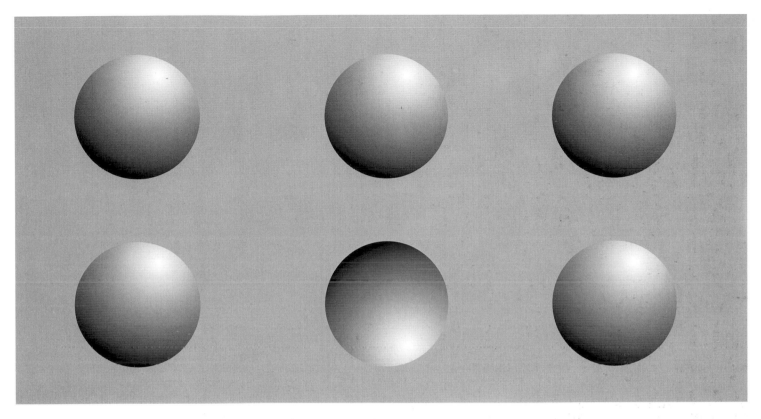

36 **Shape from Shading:** How many areas are concave? How many are convex? Turn the image upside-down and count again. Note that all the shapes change together.

GALLERY

II

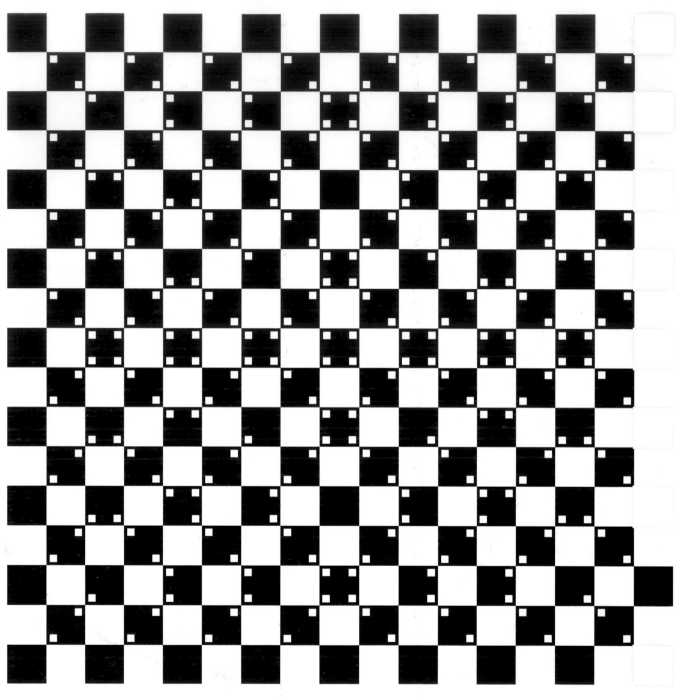

37 **Kitaoka's Waves:** *Are the lines all straight and parallel or are they bent?*

Previous page: **Monika's Cube:** *This is a lovely reversible cube by Dutch artist Monika Buch.*

Circular Poggendorf
Illusion: Are the ends of the
two circular segments perfectly
aligned?

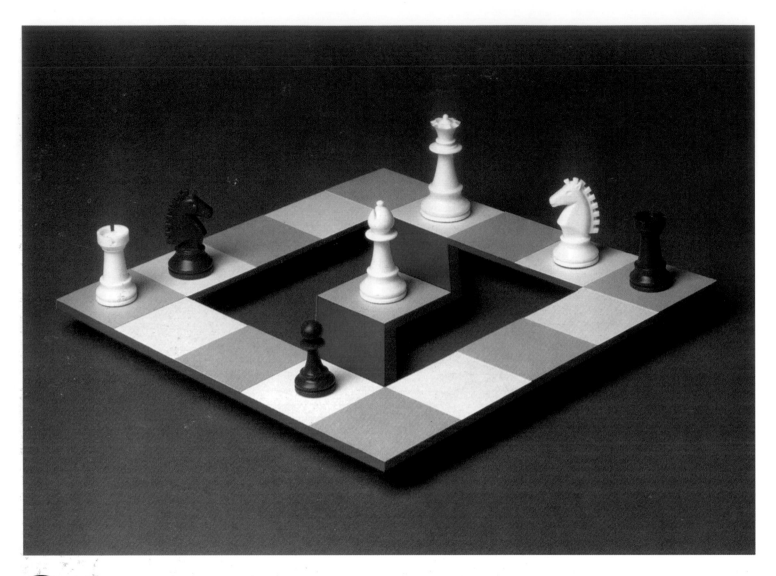

39 **Impossible Chess Set:** How is this possible?

40 **Einstein and the Sea:** *Artist Ken Knowlton creates portraits out of unusual objects. Here, Einstein is depicted using only seashells. The seashells are entirely natural and have not been painted over.*

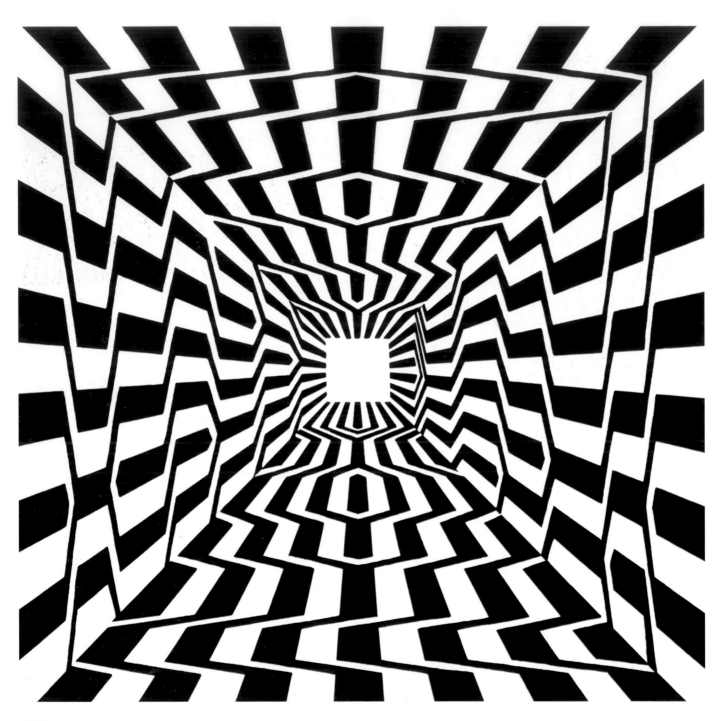

41 **Twisted Cord with Squares:** Are these perfect squares?

42 **The Müller-Lyer Illusion in Perspective:** Which red line is longer?

43 **Impossible Meander:** Follow this meandering illusion and you will see that it is impossible.

44 Ten Children: There are five heads, but one can count ten children!

45 **Boynton Illusion:** Examine these figures closely. Then step back and view them from about six feet. Do they still appear as they did close up?

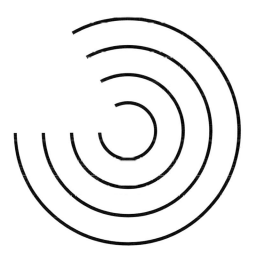

46 **Kaniza Triangle:** Do you perceive a white triangle even though there are no edges or contours? Does the triangle appear whiter than the white background?

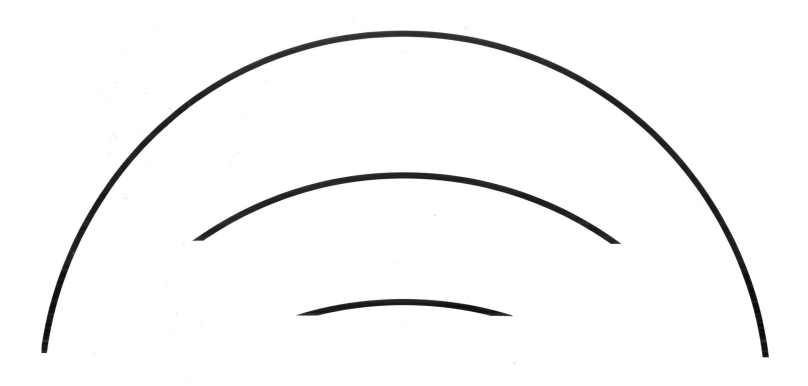

47 **Tolansky's Curvature Illusion:** Which line segment has the greatest radius of curvature?

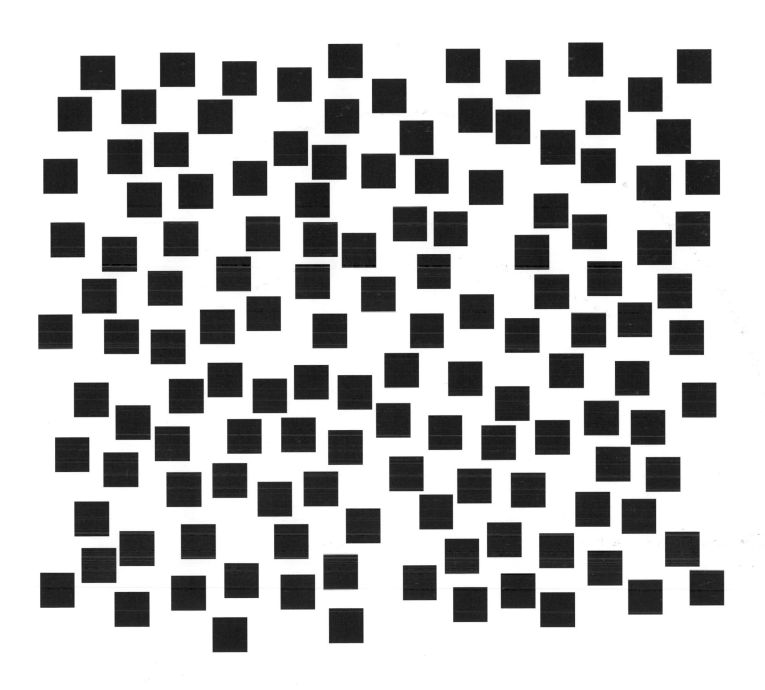

48 **Jittering Square Illusion:** Do the squares look slightly tilted in respect to each other?

49 **Where's the pie?** This scrumptious pie has the amazing ability to appear and disappear right before your eyes! You can either see one piece of pie or the whole pie with a piece missing.

50 Where's the midpoint?

One of the arcs within the circle passes through the center of the circle. Which colored line is it? Without using a measuring device can you determine the correct colored arc?

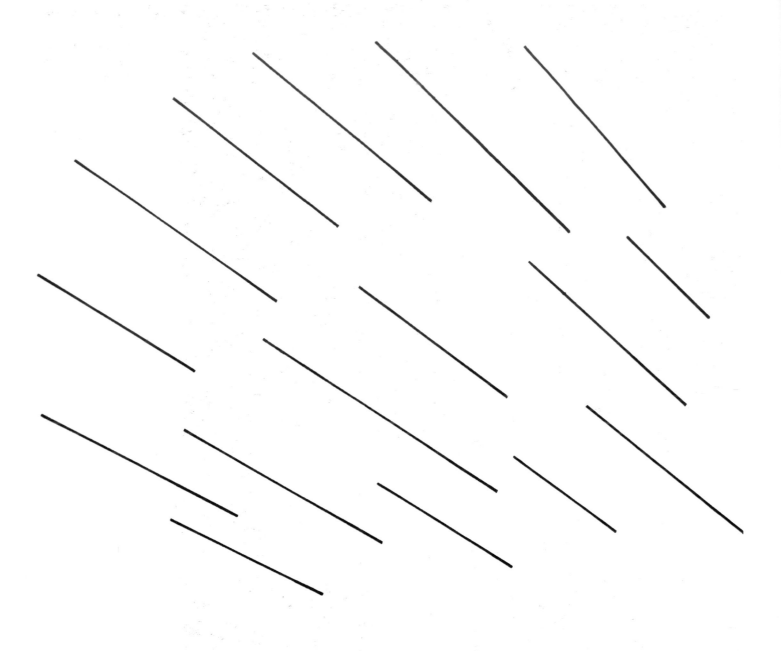

51 **Rising Line Illusion:** Can you make these lines rise out of the page? Tilt the page and look at the image with one eye from the bottom right side of the page.

52 Fruit or Portrait?
Do you see a collection of fruit or a portrait of Emperor Rudolph II?

53 Make the Lightbulb Glow

Stare at the black light bulb for thirty seconds or more without moving your gaze. Quickly transfer your gaze to a blank white or gray sheet of paper. You will see a glowing light bulb! Try it again, but this time look at a distant wall. What happens to the size of the aftereffect?

54 **Ames Room Illusion:** The two people in this room are exactly the same height!

55 **Camouflage:** What do these strange symbols signify?

56 **Time Saving Suggestion:** A wonderful figure/ground illusion by Stanford psychologist Roger Shepard.

57 **Illusionary Sphere:** Can you perceive a sphere even though there are no edges or shadows to define it?

Das gekrümmte Schachbrett

Sandro Del-Prete

60 **Ponzo Illusion:** Are the balls perfectly aligned?

61 **Height/Breadth Illusion:** Do the two stacks appear as high as they are broad?.

62 **Homage to Leonardo Da Vinci:** From where is Leonardo da Vinci obtaining his inspiration for his portrait of a mule and rider.

63 Simultaneous Orientation Contrast: Do the vertical red lines in the two center sections look tilted with respect to their surrounds?

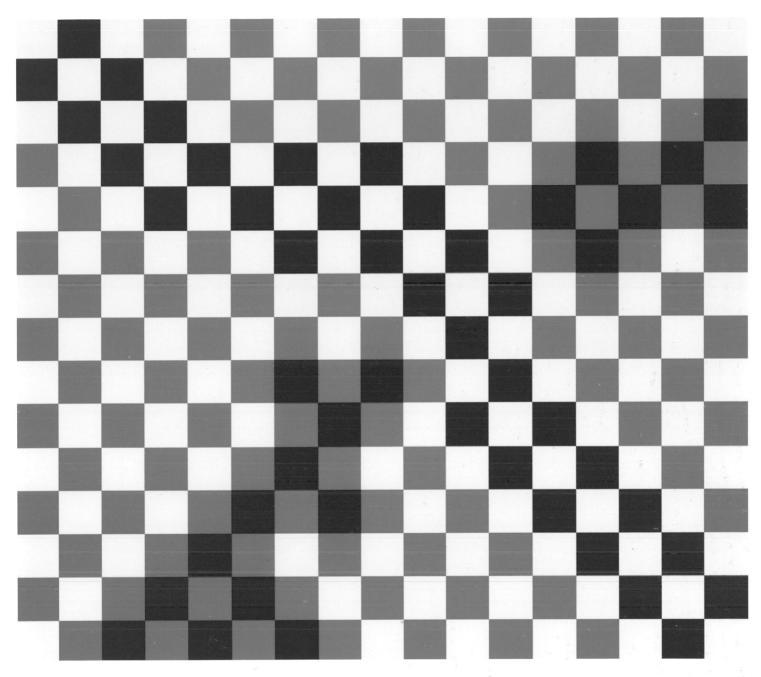

64 **Bezold Illusion:** Do all the reds appear the same?

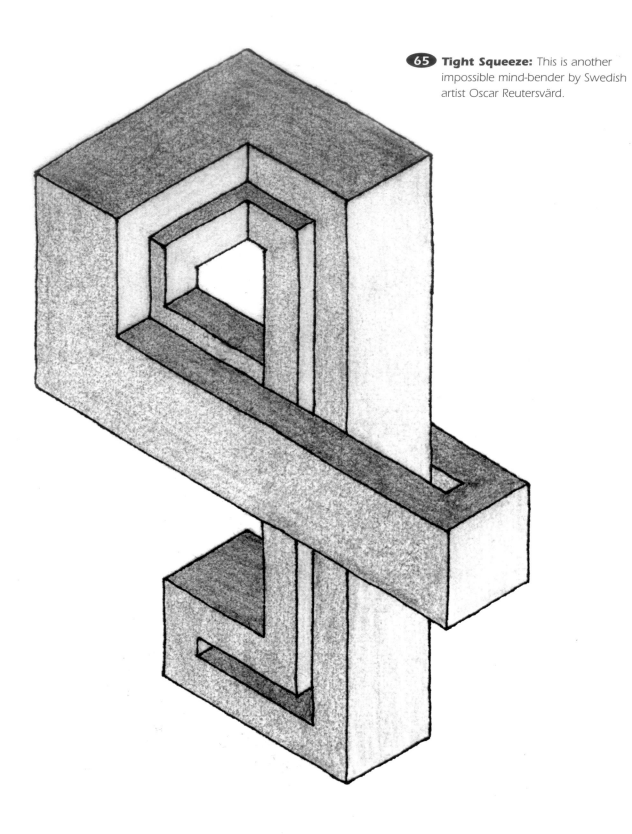

65 **Tight Squeeze:** This is another impossible mind-bender by Swedish artist Oscar Reutersvärd.

66 **Sara Nader:** Can you find the woman's face?

67 **Meandering Paradox:** This is a wonderful impossible meander by Hungarian artist Támas Farkas.

68 **Hidden Figure:** What do you see here? Try hard before looking at the answer.

69 Courtship and Matrimony:
Is this couple happy or unhappy?

70 **Egyptian-Eyezed Tête-à-tête** Do you see one face or two?

Notes on Gallery II

37. Kitaoka's Waves

Once again your eye and brain are tricking you. The lines are all perfectly straight and parallel in this new variation of the twisted cord illusion by Japanese artist and visual scientist Akiyoshi Kitaoka.

38. Circular Poggendorf Illusion

This is a perfect circle, although the ends do not appear to join together. The left curved section also appears to be slightly smaller than the right.

39. Impossible Chess Set

The chess set is entirely flat. It was created by Bruno Ernst and is based upon a design by Swedish artist Oscar Reutersvärd.

40. Einstein and the Sea

Artist Ken Knowlton creates portraits out of unusual objects. Here, Einstein is created using only seashells. Over the years a number of artists have created such portraits. The Mona Lisa is perhaps the most popular portrait recreated out of strange objects, which have included currency, stamps, little Mona Lisas, and even burnt pieces of toast.

41. Twisted Cord with Squares

The squares appear distorted, but they are all straight and parallel with each other. Bill Chessell created this op art version of the twisted cord illusion.

42. The Müller-Lyer Illusion in Perspective

Believe it or not, both red lines are exactly the same length. Perspective cues greatly enhance this version of the classic Müller-Lyer illusion. The classic version of the Müller-Lyer illusion is much weaker.

45. Boynton Illusion

Most people see the shape of the right yellow figure as defined by the squiggly line. This is known as the Boynton illusion. The edge of the squiggly figure is much stronger than the edge of the yellow figure, and at a distance the stronger edge dominates.

46. Kaniza Triangle

This effect is known as a illusory or subjective contour. The end points of the arc are interpreted as though they are disappearing under a figure, but this interpretation depends critically upon the alignment of their adjacent endpoints.

47. Tolansky's Curvature Illusion

The three arc segments appear to have widely differing curvatures, but they are all identical! The bottom two segments are just shorter arc segments of the top segment. The earliest visual receptors only interpret the world in terms of short line segments. Curvature is perceived when the relative positions of these line segments are summed across a larger area of space. So, when given a small segment of a curve, your visual system cannot detect its curvature.

48. Jittering Square Illusion

This is an example of an orientation contrast illusion. The orientation differences between two nearby edges are exaggerated, most likely by neural connections early on in the visual system. These connections sometimes enhance perceived differences to help our detection of otherwise faint objects. Psychologists Paul Snowden and Simon Watt discovered the Jittered Squares Illusion in 1998.

49. Where's the Pie?

The three-dimensional structure of the pie is ambiguous, and the 'filling' can be interpreted as belonging to either a pie or a pie slice.

50. Where's the midpoint?

Green.

51. Rising Line Illusion

In the absence of stereo information, perceived depth and three-dimensional layout is determined by pictorial cues. In this case, the pictorial depth cues are ambiguous and the lines can be interpreted as both lying flat and rising. The famous psychologist William James discovered this illusion in 1908.

52. Fruit or Portrait

Apparently the Emperor loved this portrait done c. 1590 by Italian artist Giuseppe Arcimboldo.

53. Make the Lightbulb Glow

This is called a negative aftereffect. When you look at a far wall the image should get bigger. Also, try tilting your head - the aftereffect tilts, but the room does not. This demonstrates that this effect is retinal in origin.

54. Ames Room Illusion

In fact, there are two illusions associated with an Ames Room. The first is that the room looks cubic from one special viewing point – the room really has the shape of a trapezoid, i.e., the left corner is twice as far away as the right corner and is also at a lower elevation. From a special viewing angle, however, the two corners appear to be the same distance away and the floor appears level. The second illusion, seen from the same special viewing angle, involves an apparent change in size of a person when they move from one corner to the other. The apparent shrinking is due to the change in angular size, as the person goes from the physically near corner to the physically far corner, but without approaching a visual horizon as you would if you were receding into the distance. Objects that recede into the distance approach a visual horizon. In this case, the person appears to stay on the same horizon line.

55. Camouflage

Symmetry can be a powerful and simple device to produce camouflage. Cover the left half of every symbol to reveal the answer.

57. Illusionary Sphere

The bottom edges of the cones help suggest the three-dimensional surface of the illusory sphere. Peter Tse designed this illusory three-dimensional figure.

58. The Woman with Closed Eyes

This illusion is related to the Mach band illusion, where a dark area shading into a light area appears to have greater lightness differences than actually exist: dark areas look darker, and light areas look lighter. When you stare at the woman's eyes, the differences between the dark and light areas become exaggerated, and the dark areas begins to resemble pupils.

59. Folded Chess Set

Both interpretations are possible in this drawing by Swiss artist Sandro Del Prete.

60. Ponzo Illusion

All five balls look like they are misaligned but they are all perfectly aligned. This is a variation of the Ponzo illusion.

61. Height/Breadth Illusion

Well known to fashion conscious people, vertically striped clothes tend to make the person wearing the clothes appear taller and thinner, while broad, horizontal stripes will emphasize breadth.

62. Homage to Leonardo Da Vinci

Look closely at Leonardo Da Vinci's face and then closely at the mule and rider!

63. Simultaneous Orientation Contrast

They are both vertical and parallel. It is not clear what causes this illusion, but one theory is is based on the hypothesis that there are inhibitory interactions among orientation selective neurons. In other words, the neural connections in your visual system are wired to respond more strongly to differences than to similarities in a visual scene. This can exaggerate the lines' orientations.

64. Bezold Illusion

Context can influence your perception of color. All the reds are exactly the same! This is known as the Bezold color illusion.

66. Sara Nader

Stanford psychologist Roger Shepard aptly titled this ambiguous figure/ground illusion, "Sara Nader.".

68. Hidden Figure

It is the head of a cow.

69. Courtship or Matrimony

This German 19th century topsy-turvy illustration was created by a disgruntled ex-husband or wife. The couple is perceived as being happy in "courtship," but if you turn the image upside down, you will see that the couple is unhappy in "marriage."

70. Egyptian Eyezed Tete-a-tete

If you see one face, you get a perception of depth, because the face would be behind the candlestick. Stanford psychologist Roger Shepard created this charming variation on the face/vase illusion.

71. The Margaret Thatcher Illusion

This is a facial illusion and it indicates that there is a special area of the processing of facial expressions that only works with upright faces. Because the face is upside down, this facial area is inactive. English vision scientist Peter Thompson discovered the Margaret Thatcher illusion. Only the eyes and the mouth are inverted.

71 **The Margaret Thatcher Illusion:** What is wrong with this portrait of the former British Prime minister Margaret Thatcher? Turn the photo upside down for a clue.

GALLERY

III

72 Illusion Collage: This image of basset hound was made out of a collage of animal images.

Previous page **Impossible Bird Cage:** Flemish artist Jos De Mey has created an impossible bird cage for these parrots.

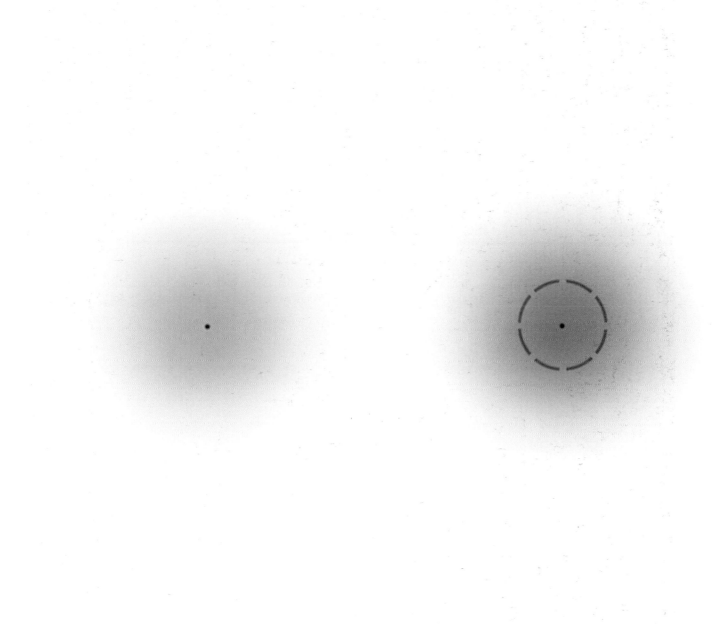

73 **Filling-in Illusion:** With one eye, stare at the center of the dot in the middle of the left smudge without moving your eye. After a few seconds the left smudge will disappear. Try this again with the center dot in the middle of the smudge on the right. This time the smudge will not disappear.

74 **Aging Illusion:** What will this young man look like when he gets older?
Turn the image upside down to find out.

75 My Wife and Mother-in-Law: Do you see the profile of a young or old woman?

76 **Shade of Napoleon:**
Can you find the standing figure of Napoleon? This figure/ground illusion appeared shortly after Napoleon's death.

77 **Illusion Causing Another Illusion:** This is a wonderful example of an illusion causing another illusion! At the intersection you will see faint, ghostly dots (Hermann Grid Illusion). These dots give rise to an impression of a series of concentric circles.

78 **Hole in Your Hand:** Create a hole in your hand! Hold a tube up to your eye. Look at something 15 feet away with both eyes (one looking through the tube). Then bring your free hand up in front of the eye that is not looking through the tube. You will see the object through a round hole in the palm of your hand! For an interesting variation, place a coin in the center of you palm and it will appear to float!

79 **Box Illusion:** Look at the figure on the outside of the cube. Which line is perpendicular to the vertical line and which line is at a slant? Cover just the outline of the cube and you will see your perception change.

80 **Marilyn Monroe Afterimage:** Stare at the image of Marilyn Monroe for thirty seconds or more without shifting your gaze. Then quickly look at a solid white or gray background. You will see her lips in red!

82 **Hermann Grid Illusion:** You will see ghostly blue dots at the intersections. If you look directly at any dot it will disappear.

83 Ponzo Illusion: Which red bar appears larger?

84 Impossible Shelf: Is this figure possible or impossible? Look closely at the shelves.

Terra Subterranea
Which figure appears larger?

86 **Persian Horses with too Many Bodies:** How many horses are here?

87 Cheshire Cat Illusion:
This is a truly amazing illusion, but it requires two people to make it work! Prop a pocket mirror vertically at the edge of a table or hold it with a steady hand. Turn it so that it reflects the scene on your right. The entire scene on your right should consist of a solid white surface. Put your face at the edge of the table and adjust your view so that your right eye sees the reflection of the white surface and your left eye looks to someone directly opposite you. You should see his/her face on a level with yours. They must remain absolutely still and not move their head. Now move your hand in a circular fashion, in front of the white surface. The face of your friend will disappear except for their mouth and eyes – just like the Cheshire Cat in *Alice in Wonderland!* You may need to try it several times, but don't give up, and allow some time to see the effect, as it is quite startling! The erasure can last for as long as five seconds if the eyes are kept stationary and there is no motion in the erased field of view. If the eyes move, the missing scene immediately reappears. If they follow the moving object, erasure does not occur.

88 Impossible Paradox: Another whimsical impossible creation by Swedish artist Oscar Reutersvärd.

89 Human Condition I:
Is the tree outside or
inside the room?

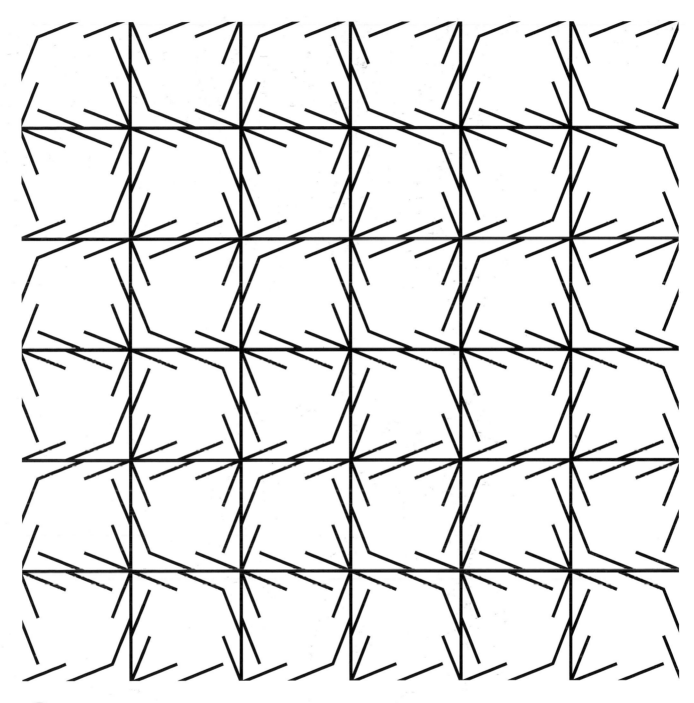

90 **Zöllner Illusion:** Do the horizontal lines appear straight and parallel? Or do they appear at an angle in respect to each other?

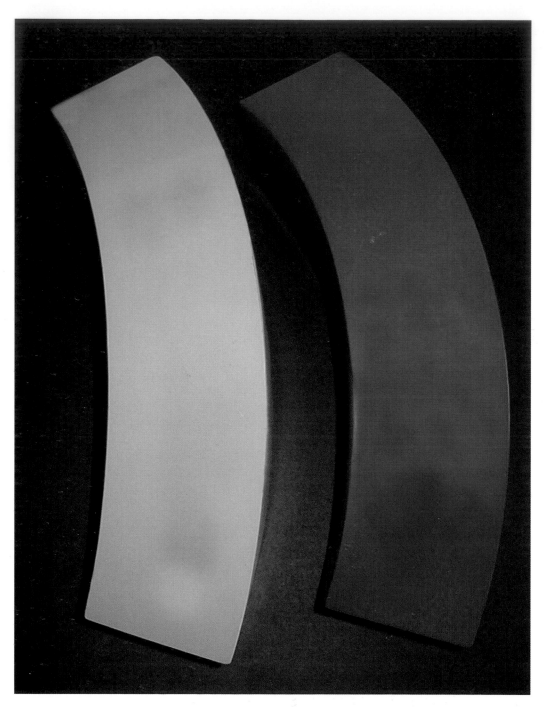

92 Clown or Circus? Here you see an illustration of a clown's face, but can you also find the circus?

93 **Rubin's Face/Vase Illusion:** Do you see a vase or two heads in profile?

96 **L'Egs-istenial Quandary:** This elephant will have trouble walking!

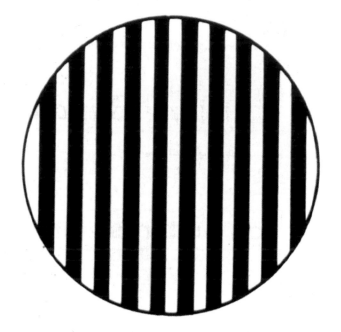

97 **Orientation Aftereffect:** Stare at the left-hand grating for thirty seconds or more without moving your gaze. Quickly stare at the right-hand grating. You should see the right-hand grating appear to bend.

98 **The Garden Fence:**
What is strange about the
slats of this fence? Cover
up either end of the fence
to see something strange.

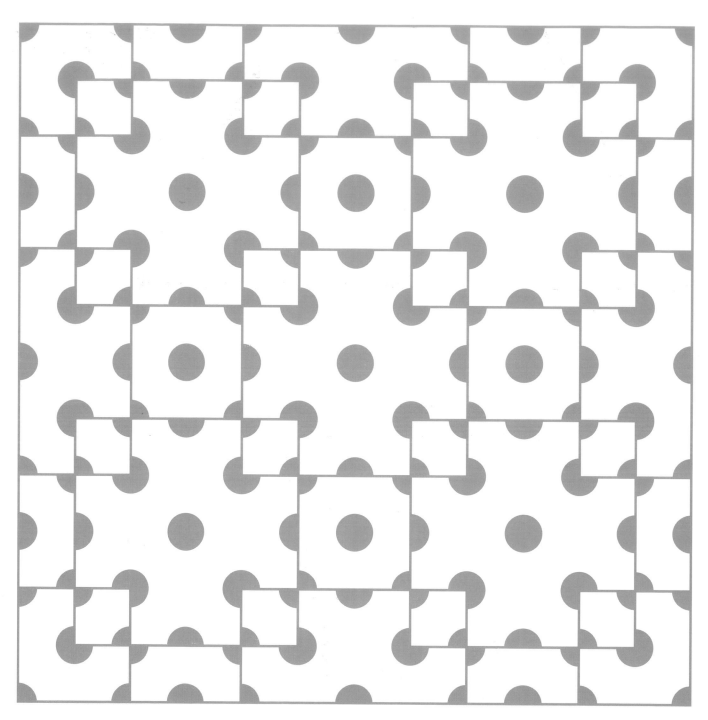

99 **Kitaoka's Distorted Square Illusion:** Do the squares appear slightly distorted?

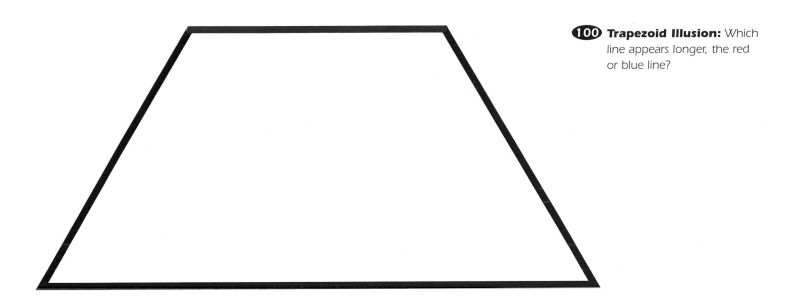

100 **Trapezoid Illusion:** Which line appears longer, the red or blue line?

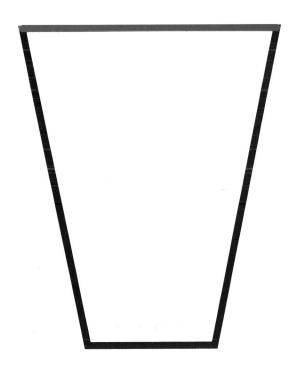

101 **Illusory Torus:** Do you see a white doughnut even though there are no edges, shadows, or contours to define it?

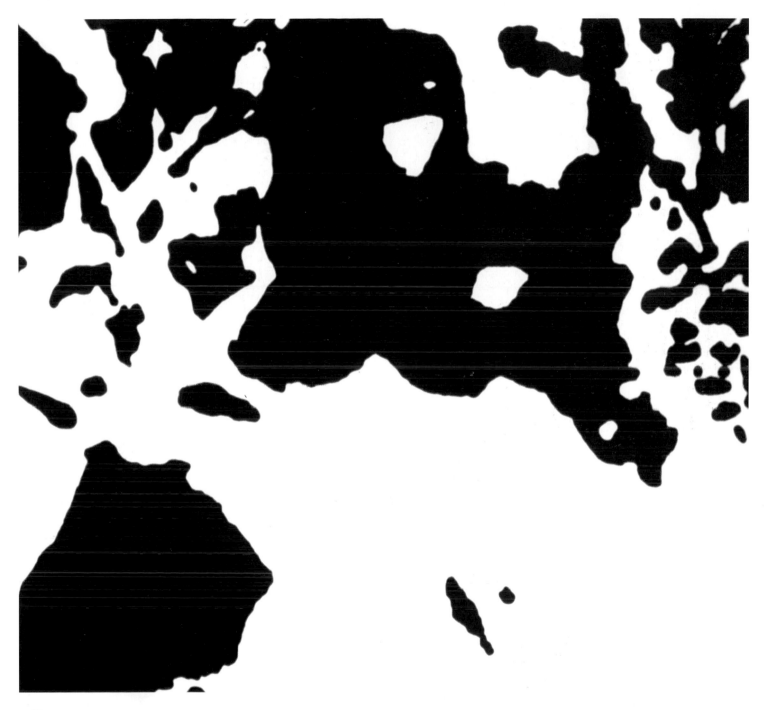

102 **Hidden Figure:** What do you see here?

103 **Mule and Jockey Puzzle:** This is one of the best puzzles of all time. Cut out the three pieces. The trick is to get the rider to mount both animals at the same time without overlapping the two larger pieces. The horses should break into a gallop when it is correctly assembled.

104 **Corporal Violet:** Can you find the three profiles hidden between the leaves?

105 Gesture of a Dancer.
Both the hand and the dancer show grace of movement in this ambiguous drawing by Swiss artist Sandro Del Prete.

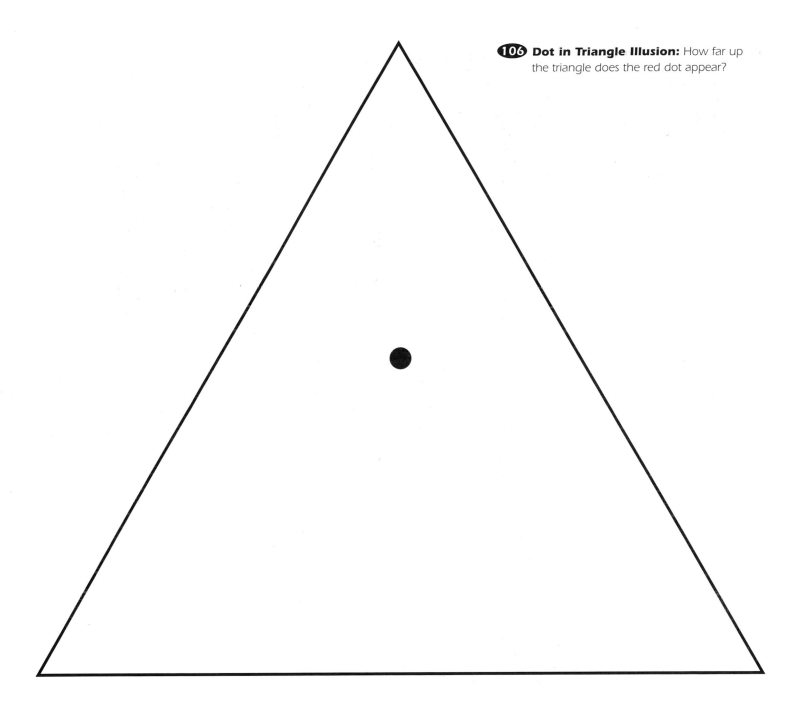

106 Dot in Triangle Illusion: How far up the triangle does the red dot appear?

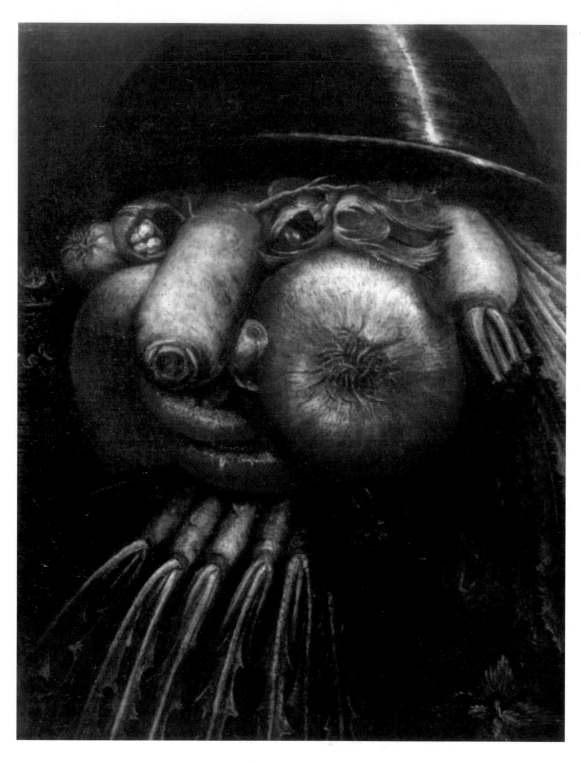

107 First Topsy-Turvy: In one orientation you will see a portrait and in another a bowl of fruit.

108 Distorted Circle Illusion: These don't appear to be perfect circles or are they?

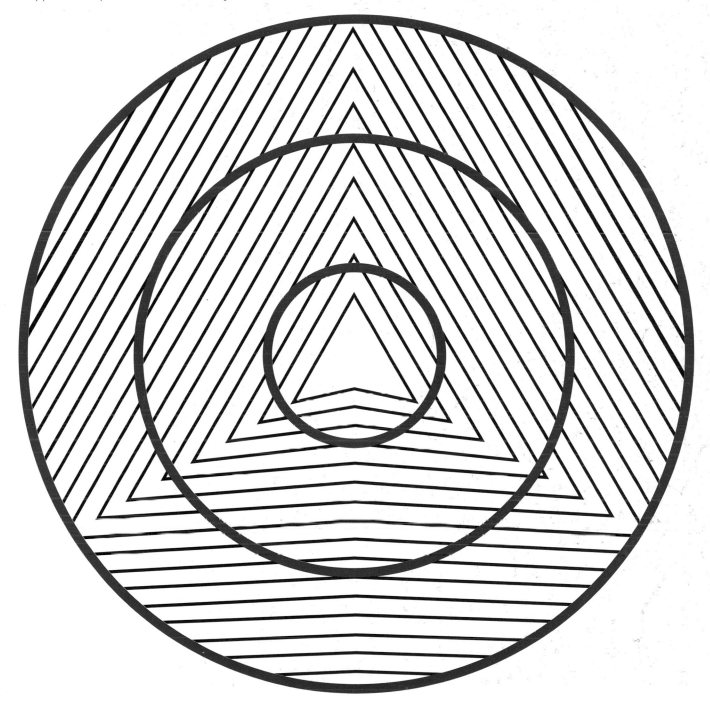

Notes on Gallery III

73. Filling-in Illusion
Your visual system only responds to the presence of change in a visual scene. Your eyes are constantly making tiny eye movements, which help to keep the visual scene changing and thus visible. In the left figure, your eye movements change the position of the center dot, but that dot by itself is too small to affect most of the smudge. In the right figure, your eye movements cause the entire dotted circle to move and its size allows most of the smudge to be refreshed.

74. Aging Illusion
Rex Whistler created this topsy-turvy portrait.

75. My Wife and Mother-in-Law
Both interpretations are possible. This classic illusion demonstrates how your visual system tends to group features based upon what you expect to see. The American psychologist Edwin Boring made this classic illusion of perceptual ambiguity popular. Boring adapted the figure from a popular 19th century puzzle trading card.

76. Shade of Napoleon
He is hiding in between the trees. The outlines of the inner trunks of the trees form the standing figure of Napoleon.

77. Illusion Causing Another Illusion
Vision scientist and op artist Nicholas Wade created this wonderful illusion causing an illusion.

78. Hole in Your Hand
Your visual system fuses the images from both eyes, resulting in the hole in the hand.

79. Box Illusion
The perspective cues of the box provide a context for the orientation of the line segments of the central figure. Remove the box and your visual system must use another context. This is known as the box illusion.

80. Marilyn Monroe Afterimage
This effect is known as a colored afterimage. When you stare at any color, you will briefly get its complimentary color in an afterimage.

81. Triangle Extent Illusion
The green line appears to be longer than the red line, although they are both identical in length.

82. Hermann Grid Illusion
This is a coloured variation of the Hermann Grid Illusion. If you make the squares black then you will see ghostly gray dots at the intersections. These ghostly dots arise as a side-effect of how the neural circuitry in the retina operates.

83. Ponzo Illusion
Both bars are identical in size, although the inner bar appears to be larger. This is known as the Ponzo illusion. This perspective illusion is greatly enhanced by the two center radiating lines.

84. Impossible Shelf
It's impossible.

85. Terra Subterranea
The background figure appears to be larger than the foreground figure even though they are both identical in size. If you could somehow move the background figure to the same level as the foreground figure the illusion would no longer work. Stanford psychologist Roger Shepard created this perspective illusion.

86. Persian Horses with too Many Bodies
Count the heads and then count the bodies. This ambiguous illusion was created in Persia sometime during the 17th century.

87. Cheshire Cat Illusion
The image you see is actually the combination of two different images; you notice your friend's face because it is more interesting than the white wall. When you move your hand, your visual system replaces portions of your friend's face with white because the motion of your hand suddenly draws more attention to the white wall. Sally Duensing of the Exploratorium, an excellent hands-on science museum in San Francisco, discovered the Cheshire Cat illusion.

89. Human Condition I
In 'Human Condition I'. Flemish artist René Magritte was determined to depict the ambiguity that exists between a real object, one's mental image of it, and its painted representation.

90. Zöllner Illusion
The lines are straight and parallel even though they appear to be bent. This is another variant of the classic Zöllner illusion.

91. Wundt Block Illusion
They are identical. This illusion still works when you hold them in your hands.

92. Clown or Circus?
Turn the illustration on its side. Artist Larry Kettlekamp created this charming topsy-turvy illusion.

93. Rubin's Face/Vase Illusion
One can see both interpretations. At any time, however, you can only see either the faces or the vase. If you continue looking, the figure may reverse itself several times so that you alternate between seeing the faces and the vase. The Gestalt psychologist Edgar Rubin made this classic figure/ground illusion famous. Rubin had drawn his inspiration for this illusion from a 19th century puzzle card.

94. Wade's Spiral
English vision scientist and op artist Nicholas Wade gives us his version of the Fraser Spiral illusion. Although it looks like a spiral, it is really a series of concentric circles.

95. Sister Rivals
This illusion by Roger Shepard is called 'Sister Rivals'. The only way it really makes sense is if you see two people.

97. Orientation Aftereffect
This illusion is known as a tilt aftereffect. It occurs because the orientation detectors in your retinas become fatigued and its signal becomes much weaker relative to other orientation detectors.

99. Kitaoka's Distorted Square Illusion
The squares are perfect. This is another op art variation on the twisted cord illusion by Japanese artist and vision scientist Akiyoshi Kitaoka.

100. Trapezoid Illusion
The red line appears slightly longer than the blue line, even though they are both identical in length. Angles of less than 90 degrees make the enclosed line appear shorter while angles of more than 90 degrees make it appear longer. This is known as the trapezoid illusion.

101. Illusory Torus
Peter Tse provided the inspiration for this three dimensional illusory contour figure.

102. Hidden Figure
You will see the face of a bearded man.

103. Mule and Jockey Puzzle
The great American master of puzzles Sam Lloyd created this wonderful puzzle. The solution involves an illusion! The bodies of the mules are ambiguous.

106. Dot in Triangle Illusion
The red dot is located exactly halfway up the triangle, although it appears to be much higher. This is a variation of the upside-down T illusion.

107. First Topsy-Turvy
This topsy-turvy illusion by 16th century Italian artist Giuseppe Arcimboldo is the earliest attempt at a topsy-turvy illusion known.

108. Distorted Circle Illusion
The perfect circles appear distorted when placed on top of this background. This is another example of an orientation contrast illusion, where each pair of intersecting lines appear more perpendicular to each other than they physically are.

109. Flowering of Love
Swiss artist Sandro Del Prete created this romantic and ambiguous illusion.

109 **Flowering of Love:** Can you see the two lovers in the rose petals?

GALLERY
IV

110 White's Illusion: Do the gray vertical bars appear identical or different?

Previous page **Arcturus II:** Do you see four Xs in each colored pattern? The Xs are an illusion.

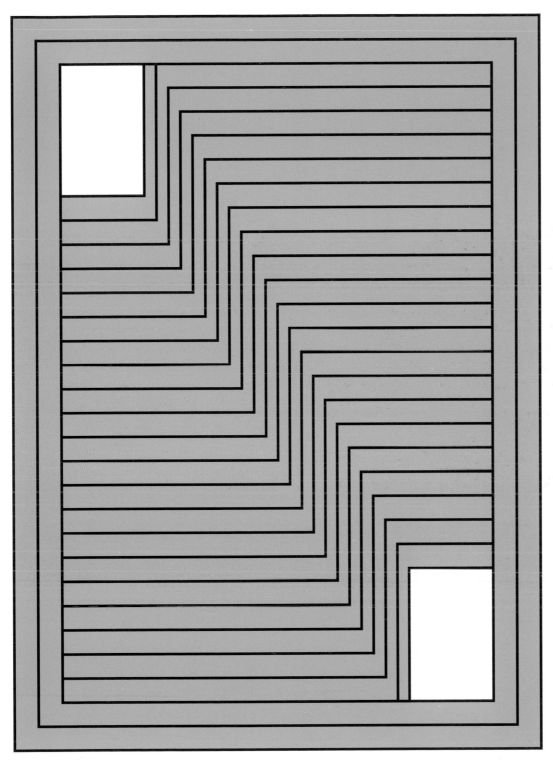

111 **Thiery's Figure:**
Where is the white square located?

112 **Gazing Illusion:** The two men appear to be looking in different directions. Cover up everything below their eyes and you will see them gazing in exactly the same direction.

113 **Verbeek's Topsy-Turvy Cartoon:**
Turn this image upside down and you will
see another scene.

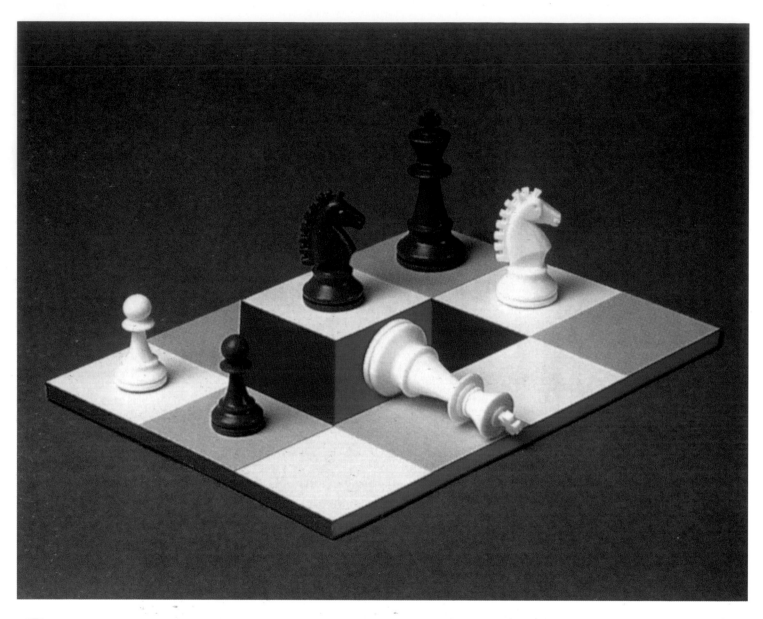

114 Chess set: How is this chess set possible? Can you tell how it was made?

115 Twisted Circles. This is a series of perfect concentric circles! This is an example of a twisted cord illusion

116 **St. George and the Dragon:** Can you find both a portrait of St. George and a depiction of his slaying of the dragon?

117 **E Puzzle:** Cut out the three pieces and arrange them to form the letter E. The solution just might prove illusory.

118 **Muscular Aftereffect:** This is a fun jogging illusion that you can do with a friend. Have your friend run on the treadmill for about three minutes while blindfolded. Quickly help them off the treadmill and ask them to run in place, while still blindfolded. They will run forward, even though they think they are running in place.

119 **Minimum Visible:** If you look closely at this image you will see only dots. If you back away and look at it from just the right angle you may see a face.

120 **Hering Figure:** Do the black lines appear to be bowed out?

121 **Glee turns Glum:** One moment they are happy and in another moment they are sad. You can switch their moods by inverting the image.

122 **Neptune:** Can you find the invisible figure of Neptune guarding the sea?

123 **Zollner.** Are the thick black lines and the open spaces between them exactly parallel to one another? Look again.

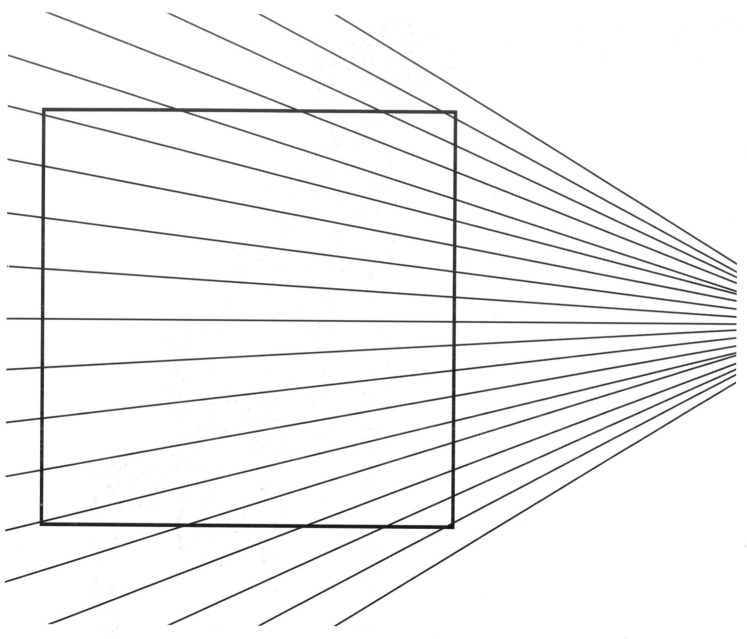

124 **Orbison Illusion:** Does this square appear distorted?

125 Larger within Smaller: What is the impossibility that is depicted in this drawing by Swedish artist Oscar Reutersvärd?

126 Illusory wedges: Do you perceive wedges?

127 Incident on a Railway Bridge:
Are these trains going to collide?

128 Two for the Price of One!

There are two cars here! Can
you find both of them?

129 **The Plank Illusion.** Here are two men standing on a level plank. The men are the same height in the picture on the left, but on the right, the man in the red shirt is smaller. All they did was change places! This illusion is known as the plank illusion and is found in many tourist attractions.

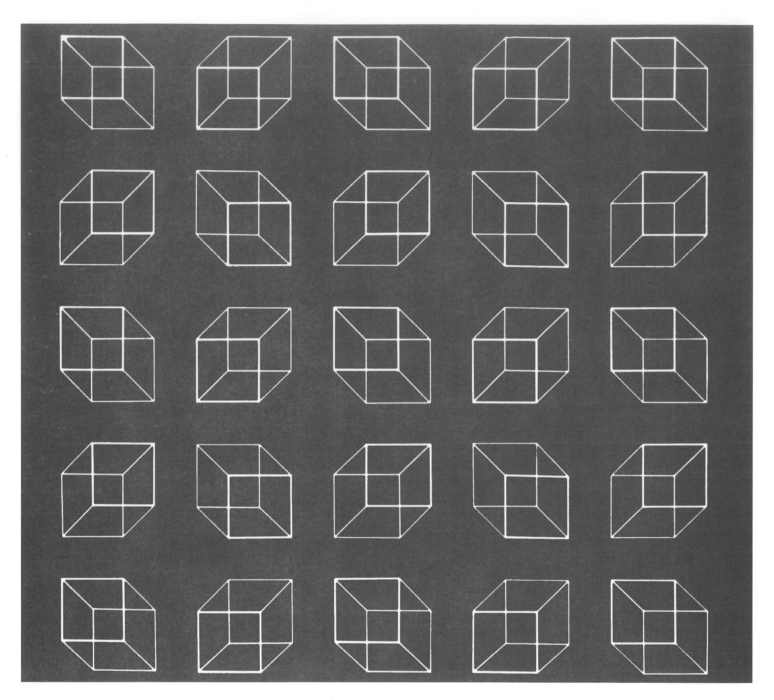

130 **Necker Cube Grouping Illusion:** Can you make all these cubes "flip-flop" at once? Can you flip-flop only one cube while looking at the entire image?

132 **Ebbinghouse Illusion:**

Do the inner circles appear to be different in size?

133 Impossible Stairway:
Can you go up any levels
when you climb this set
of stairs?

134 **It's a Miracle!** Look at this illustration with both eyes and bring it slowly to your face. The hands will touch!

135 Impossible Fork:

How many prongs can you count? Cover up each half and you will find that each end is perfectly possible, but when you uncover the two possible halves you will end up with an impossible figure. No one knows who first created this famous impossible figure, which started appearing in various publications during the year 1964.

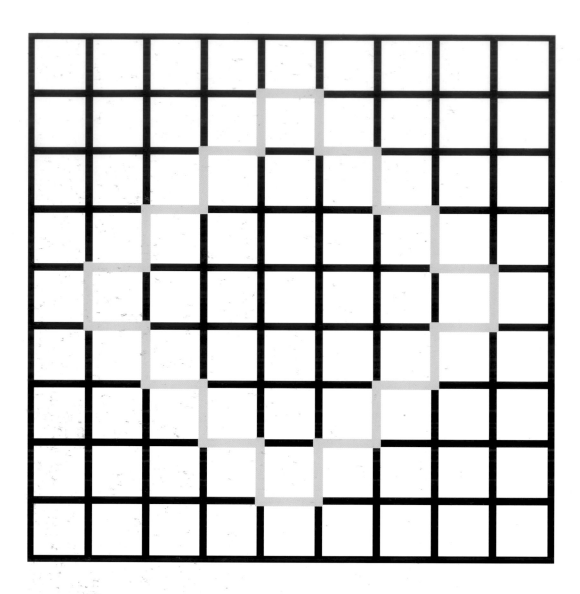

136 Van Tuiji Illusion: Do the inside squares of the bounded blue lines appear to have a faint bluish tint?

137 Natural camouflage. Can you find the American Bittern and its nest hiding in the swamp?

138 **Mach Illusion:** This is a fun illusion. Fold a piece of white paper as shown. Lay it down on the table and view it with only one eye from a distance above. Because of contradictory depth cues the paper will "invert." You should see the paper appear to stand upright. If you can hold this image stable and move from side to side the paper will appear to follow you. It should also change in brightness.

139 **Tricked You:** Is the red square larger than the blue square or does it just appear that way? Are the horizontal lines straight?

140 **Nature's Most Beautiful Illusion:** A rainbow is surely nature's most beautiful illusion. Next time you see a rainbow, try to find the fainter secondary and tertiary bows.

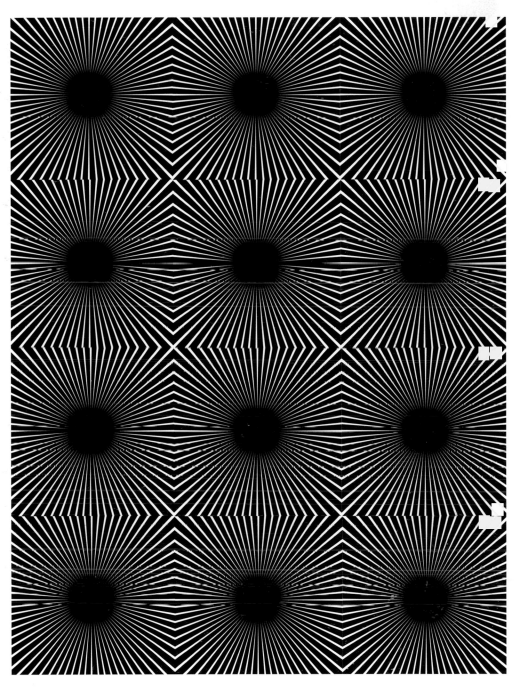

141 **Illusory Movement:** Shake this figure and you will see illusory movement.

Notes on Gallery IV

Arcturus II (Page 123)
Each concentric square is of uniform reflectance. The corners of each square appear brighter because two of the sides border a darker area in an effect known as simultaneous contrast. Your visual system adds the brighter corners to form straight lines in the shape of an X. "Arcturus II" is by French artist Victor Vasarely.

110. White's Illusion
The gray vertical bars are identical to each other. White's illusion is produced by a combination of two effects, grouping and simultaneous contrast. The small gray horizontal rectangles are grouped to form two large vertical gray bars. The gray bars, however, appear to be on different backgrounds. Simultaneous contrast causes the gray bar on the white background to seem darker than the gray bar on the black background.

111. Thiery's Figure
This figure will flip-flop in depth because of conflicting perspective cues. It is a variant of Thiery's figure.

113. Verbeek's Topsy-Turvy Cartoon
Gustave Verbeek published a wonderful topsy-turvy cartoon in The Sunday New York Herald in 1900. Although restricted to the normal six-panel comic strip format of his time, Verbeek was not content with this and decided to have twelve panels with no increase in space. This was achieved by having the story continue by turning the comic strip upside down. This is one illustration from his set of comical characters.

114. Chess Set
The chessboard is entirely flat, but it uses deceptive shading and coloring to give the illusion that it is not flat. Bruno Ernst constructed this chess set.

116. St. George and the Dragon
The hair of the large profile defines the battle. Swiss artist Sandro Del Prete created this wonderful ambiguous illusion.

117. E Puzzle
It forms the letter E with illusory contours.

118. Muscular Aftereffect
This is a muscular aftereffect. It is similar to the experience that some people have when exiting a long escalator.

119. Minimum Visible
Some of the dots are very slightly larger than the other dots. In those areas there is more black. Seen from a distance, the slightly blacker areas can be grouped to form the image of a face.

120. Hering Figure
They are perfectly straight and parallel. This classic illusion was discovered by the 19th century German physiologist Ewald Hering.

121. Glee turns Glum
Created by Roger Shepard

122. Neptune
The fish, dolphins and plants form the outline of Neptune. This is a very nice example of an illusion that flip-flops in meaning. The drawing is by Swiss artist Sandro Del Prete.

124. Orbison Illusion
This is really a perfect square; however, radiating lines can distort one's perception of lines and shapes. Although this illusion is known as the Orbison illusion, it is a variation of the Hering illusion.

125. Larger Within Smaller
There are larger pieces fitting within smaller ones!

126. Illusory Wedges
The wedges are illusory. This is another variation on the twisted cord illusion by Japanese op artist and vision scientist Akiyoshi Kitaoka.

127. Incident on a Railway Bridge
How can the trains collide in a drawing! This is another fun impossible scene by Swiss artist Sandro Del Prete.

128. Two for the Price of One!
One car is on top of the other car.

129. The Plank Illusion
The plank is absolutely level and the camera position and controls are the same for both exposures. It is a misleading sloping background that causes this illusion augmented by the fact that the camera is slightly off-center

130. Necker Cube Grouping Illusion
You should be able to "reverse" all the cubes, because your visual system tends to group like items together. It is much more difficult to "flip-flop" a single cube when looking at the entire set of cubes.

131. Duck/Rabbit
Both interpretations are possible in this classic illusion created by psychologist Joseph Jastrow around 1900.

132. Ebbinghouse Illusion
The inner circles are identical in size. When larger circles surround the middle circle, it appears smaller than the circle surrounded by dots. This is known as the Ebbinghouse or Titchner illusion.

133. Impossible Stairway
You will always remain at the same level when you climb this set of stairs. Swedish artist Oscar Reutersvärd, who is generally regarded as the "father of impossible figures", created this impossible figure.

135. Impossible Fork
When you look at this figure, you first calculate contours or outlines, and from this you try to perceive the boundary of the shape. Your visual system's confusion occurs because several contours of this figure are ambiguous. For example, this figure makes use of the fact that a cylinder can be represented by a pair of lines, while a rectangular bar requires three lines. The illusion is contructed by completing each pair of lines to make a cylinder at one end, and each triplet to make a square bar at the other end.

This ambiguity makes the figure violate another basic distinction, that between flat and curved surfaces, where a flat strip twists into a cylindrical surface. The figure, furthermore, gives contradictory cues for the depth estimation for the position of the middle prong. And finally, there is a counting paradox associated with the figure – two prongs into three prongs.

136. Van Tuiji Illusion
All the squares bounded by the blue lines are absolutely white. Vision scientist Van Tuiji discovered this example of neon color spreading in 1975.

137. Natural Camouflage
This is an example of a natural illusion camouflage. The Bittern even mimics the movement of the reeds in the background to avoid being spotted.

138. Mach Illusion
The card follows you because of a reversed motion parallax. Motion parallax is what you observe when you look outside the window of a moving car. Objects that are close to you move quickly and in the opposite direction to your movement. Objects that are further away appear to move slower and also in the opposite direction. In the case of this illusion, the nearest and farthest points are reversed, which causes a reverse in the motion parallax. This illusion was discovered by the physicist Ernst Mach in the 19th century and is known as the Mach illusion.

139. Tricked You
The lines are bent and the red square is bigger. If you answered that they were the same size and that the horizontal lines were straight, you were tricked, because there is no illusion. However, if you were tricked, you were fooled into an illusion without an illusion! This, of course, is an illusion!

142. Hogarth
There are over twenty mistakes of perspective in this 17th century illustration by William Hogarth.

142 **Hogarth:** How many mistakes of perspective can you find?

GALLERY
V

143 **What is this?** Can you make sense of this bizarre scene? The photograph has not been altered.

Previous page: **Enigma:** Stare at the circles and you will perceive motion occurring within the rings. They can suddenly change direction too.

144 **A Two Bodied Woman:** To which body does Lady Bird Johnson's head belong in this unaltered photograph?

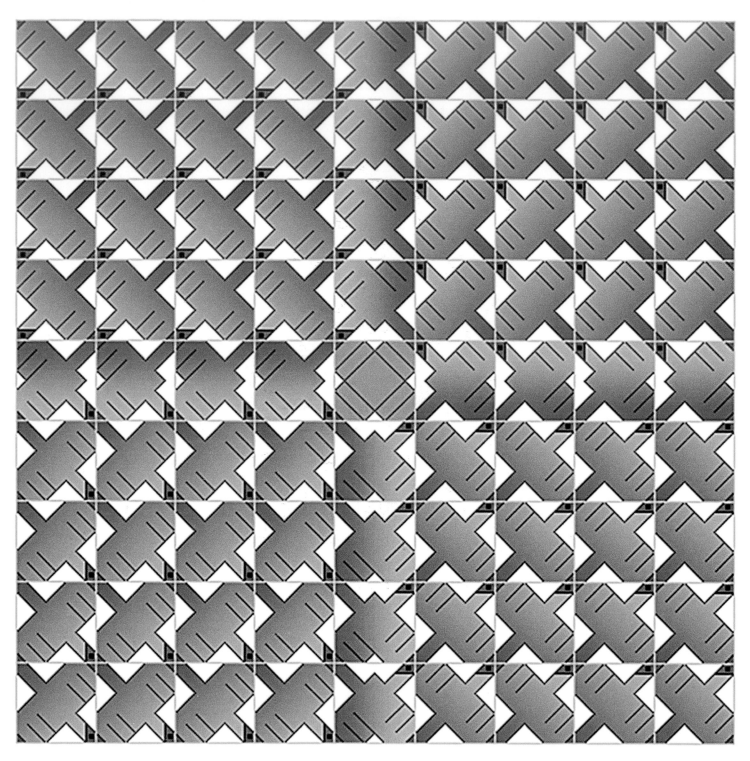

145 **The Café Escher Illusion:** Do the squares appear to bulge in the center? Check them with a straight edge. Japanese artist and vision scientist Akiyoshi Kitaoka created this new illusion, which he calls the Café Escher illusion.

146 **The Presidential Illusion:** How fast can you identify the famous politicians in this photograph? Carefully examine the picture again. You might be in for a surprise!

148 **Between Illusion and Reality:** Look carefully at the two openings. Is this construction physically possible? Try covering the top half of the illustration, examine it, and then separately cover the bottom half. What happens? Swiss artist Sandro Del Prete created this impossible scene, which takes place somewhere between Illusion and Reality.

149 **The Floating Vase:** This vase appears to be floating off the ground, but is it really?

150 Misaligned Eyes: Do the eyes appear to be misaligned? Check them with a straight edge.

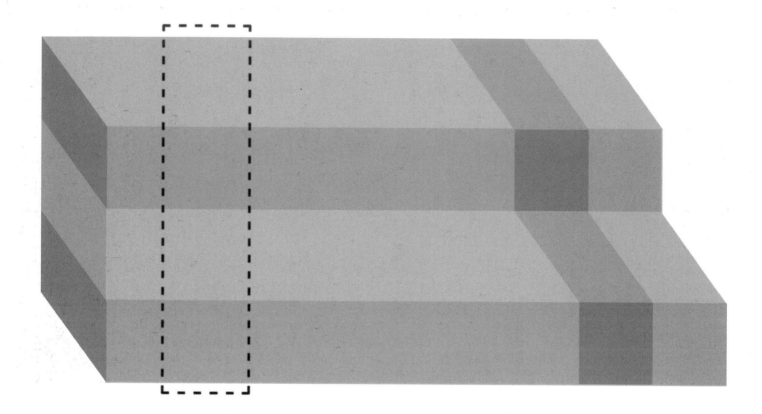

151 **Reflectance Illusion:** There are two illusions in this image by MIT vision scientist Ted Adelson. The stairs look like stacked planks on the left side, but like steps on the right side, which is an impossible construction.

Secondly, there is a reflectance illusion: the dark and light sections on the ends of the left 'planks' are the same color as the gray stripe running down the steps on the right.

152 Moretti's Impossible Blocks: Believe it or not, these seemingly different sculptures are three different views of the same sculpture!

Photo A

From this angle, you will see a set of blocks based on a design by Swedish artist Oscar Reutersvärd – three vertically aligned blocks at the top, which somehow merge into two vertically aligned blocks on the bottom. This construction is impossible.

Photo B

Turn the sculpture clockwise by 90 degrees and you will see a set of several horizontally aligned impossible blocks, also based on a design by Oscar Reutersvärd.

Photo C

The third view shows the sculpture from an angle midway between the other two. Italian artist Guido Moretti created this remarkable impossible transforming bronze sculpture.

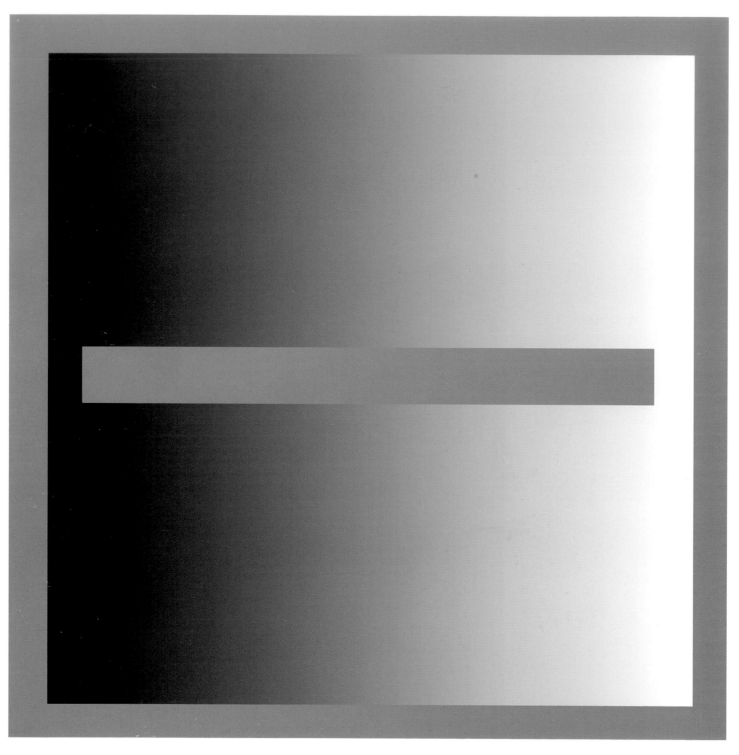

153 **Simultaneous Contrast Illusion:** Is the horizontal bar the same shade of gray throughout? Check by covering everything except the horizontal bar.

Photo A

Without using a measuring device, which angle appears the largest? Which angle appears the smallest? Arrange the angles in order of descending order of angular size if you can.

Photo B

Do all the angles appear to be the same size?

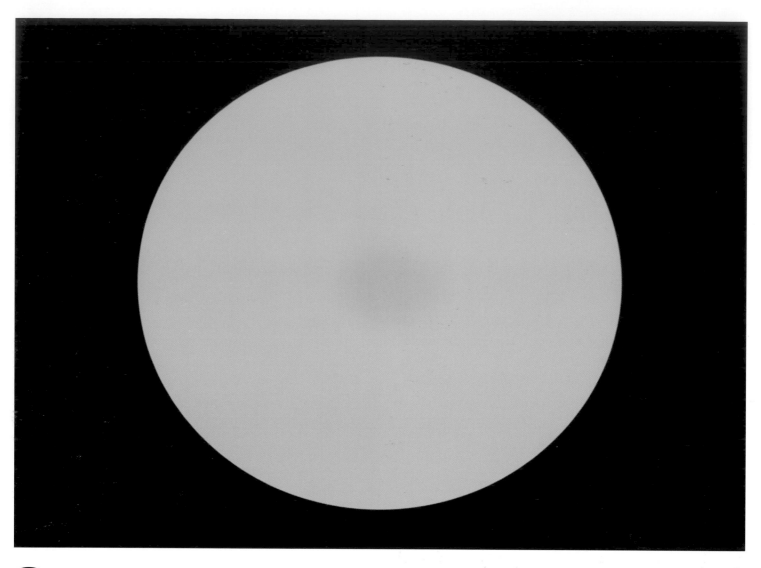

155 Filling-in Illusion: Stare at the blue dot in the center of the image, without averting your gaze or attention, and it will gradually fade out. This is a filling-in illusion.

156 Duet: A pianist transforms into a violinist in this sculpture by Japanese artist Shigeo Fukuda.

157 **Revolving Circles:** Focus on the dot in the center and move your head (or the book) backwards and forwards. The inner circle should rotate. Try also slowly turning the page.

158 **Leonardo Anamorphosis:** In this painting by Hans Hamngren, the square in the center is blank. When a pyramid-shaped mirror is placed on the square and you look straight down on it (as shown), you see the portrait of Leonard Da Vinci. This Dutch artist created this anamorphic portrait as a homage to Leonardo Da Vinci, who created the first anamorphic image, c. 1500.

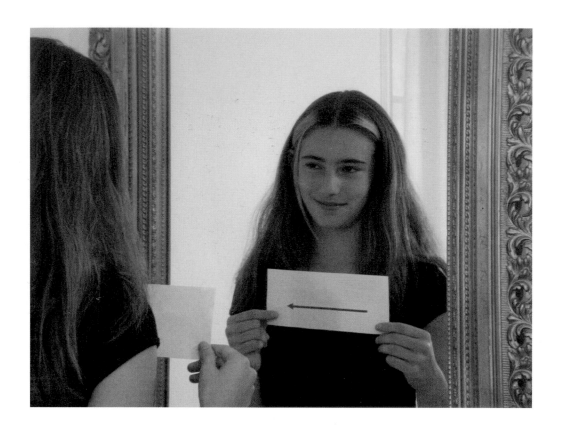

159 **The Mirror Paradox:** This is an old paradox about a mirror. When you look in a mirror it reverses the side your hair is parted on. The image in the mirror is left and right reversed, but not top-to-bottom reversed. The image in the mirror reverses left and right, but not top and bottom. Why?

Another way to look at the problem is to lie down on your side and look into the mirror. Your hair will still part on the left side. Your left and right used to be respectively up and down and the up and the down were previously right and left. So, how did the mirror 'figure out' what you were going to do?

English vision scientist Richard Gregory offers an experiment using a match and its box. Hold a match horizontal and parallel to a vertical mirror. What happens? When the head of the match is to the right, its head is also to the right. It is not left-right reversed. However, the writing on the matchbox, when viewed in the mirror, is left-right reversed. So, it appears as if the match and its box behave differently! Why is this?

160 **A Taste Illusion:** Here is a fun taste illusion. Prepare some slices of an apple and a pear. Blindfold your subject and ask him to hold his nose. Place a piece of apple on his tongue. Let him chew it. Can he distinguish apple from pear? Between trials have him rinse his mouth with plain water.

Repeat the experiment. This time he should be blindfolded and not hold his nose. Can he distinguish apple from pear with his nose or with his tongue and mouth? If you hold a slice of pear beneath his nose while he eats an apple, which does he think he's eating?

161 Kitaoka's Spiral: This appears to be a spiral, but it is really a series of concentric circles. What happens when you cover half the illustration?

162 World of Worlds: A world made of worlds by American artist Jerry Downs.

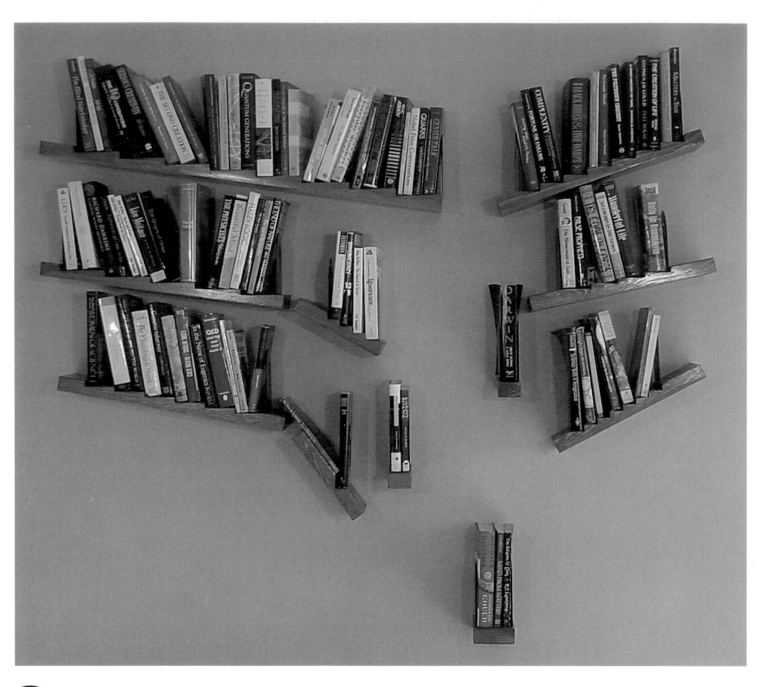

163 Falling Bookcase This bookcase, built by the author, appears to be falling. It is based on an original design by Ron Christenton.

164 **An Ambulance in an Inside-Out World:**

Photo A
This toy ambulance does not look too unusual; however, compare it with the photograph below.

Photo B
The ambulance is really inside out! The inside of the ambulance was painted to look like the outside of the ambulance.

165 Cat and Mouse Playing Hide and Seek: Is the cat hiding from the mouse or the mouse hiding from the cat? English artist Peter Brookes created this charming ambiguous figure ground illusion.

166 **Breakfast Before and After:** Can you spot at least two items that are unusual in this breakfast scene? One is easy, while the other is a bit harder.

167 **Magical Chinese Pool:** There is a 'magical pool' inside the Plum Temple located in Zhaoqing, near Guangzhou in China. It was built around 996 AD and has been baffling visitors for over 1000 years!

Photo A

If you stand on the right side of the pool and look to the left, the pool appears to get increasingly shallower.

Photo B

If you stand on the opposite side of the pool, it now appears as if the left end of the pool is deep and gets shallower to the right. This is the opposite of what you saw in the previous image.
How is this possible?

168 **Miracle at the Parthenon:** Is this a miracle? This is an unaltered photograph of one of nature's most beautiful illusions – the rainbow. How did the photographer capture this image of a rainbow on top of the Greek Parthenon? Was it just a matter of luck, or was it something else?

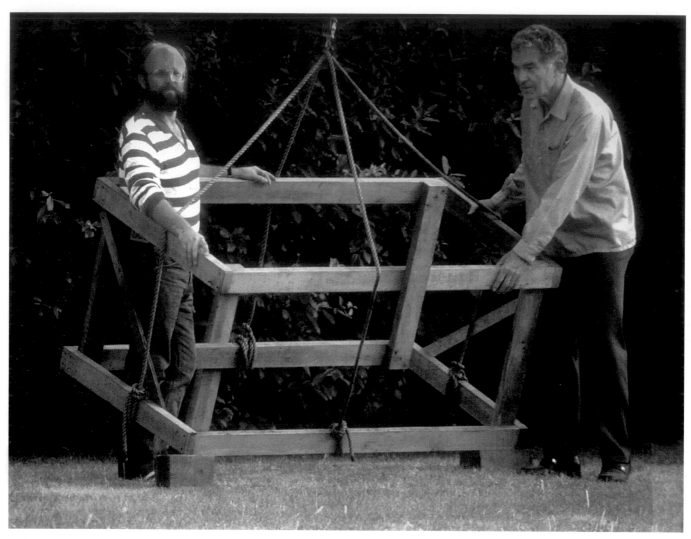

169 **Jerry Andrus' Crazy Crate:**

Photo A

American magician Jerry Andrus has created a 'Crazy Crate.' How did he manage to connect the straight vertical support beams in such an impossible way? Look at the photograph on the next page to see how he did it.

Photo B
Here the 'Crazy Crate' is seen from another angle, which reveals its true construction.

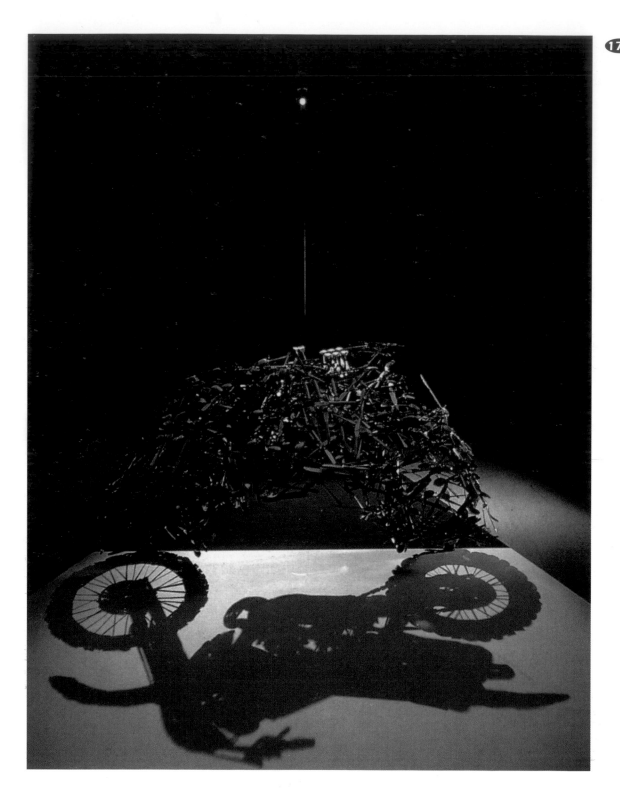

170 Shadow of a Motorcycle: Japanese artist Shigeo Fukuda arranged forks, spoons and knives to cast a shadow of a motorcycle.

171 **The Magical Mask of Noh:** The Japanese Noh mask trick dates back to the Kamakura era (1192–1333). The rigid mask was thought to be possessed, because of its 'magical' ability to change expression.

Photo A
Here you see the rigid mask straight on. Compare its facial expression with the two photographs below to see how it changes its expression depending on how the mask is tilted.

Photo B

Photo C

Photo A

This engraving depicts a scene from Jules Verne's 19th century novel *The Mysterious Island*. Hungarian artist Istvan Orosz hid a portrait of Jules Verne somewhere in this image. It needs, however, a reflective cylinder to see it. Look at the picture on the next page to see the portrait revealed.

Photo B

When a reflective cylinder is placed at a specific point on the image, you will see the portrait of Jules Verne reflected onto the cylinder.

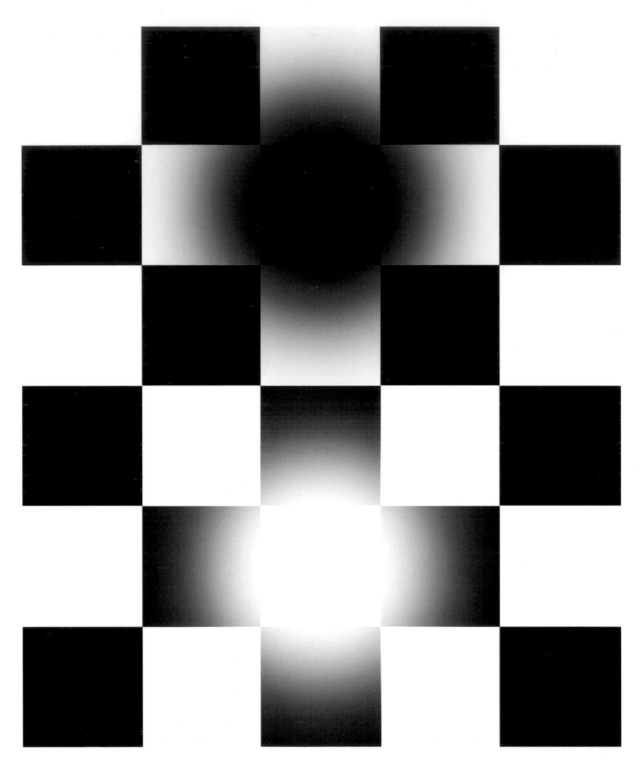

173 **Brightness Illusion:** Do the black and white squares at the centers of the 'clouds' appear to be different in brightness to their respective counterpart squares?

174 Cross-Modal Illusion: Most people would be surprised to learn that one sense can dramatically influence another. For example, it would be surprising to learn that sound can dramatically influence one's visual perception of an event. Here is an interesting description of one such cross-modal illusion.

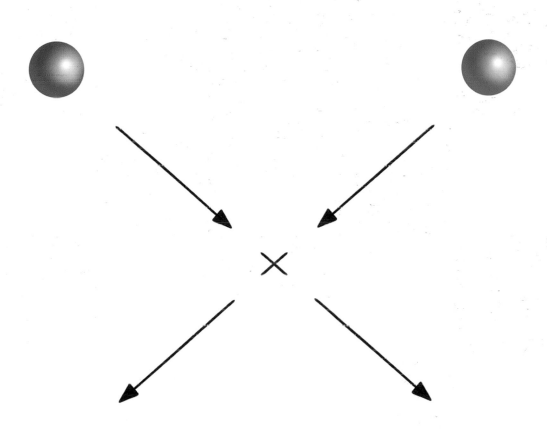

The ball at the top left moves at a constant rate to the bottom right. An identical ball, starting from the top right, moves simultaneously and at the same rate, to the bottom left. They pass through one another at 'X'. This is the motion you perceive unless you make a 'colliding' sound when the balls merge at 'X'. Then you perceive the balls as colliding where the ball that started at the top left ends up at the bottom left and the other ball that started at the top right ends at the bottom right.

Notes on Gallery V

Enigma (Page 159)
Fixation on the center induces in most, though not all, people a strong perception of motion occurring within the rings. The motion is in opposite directions in different rings and can change direction in any one ring during one viewing. French artist Isia Leviant created this image and titled it 'Enigma', because scientists were mystified about why the effect occurs. Semir Zeki, a neuroscientist at University College, London took PET brain scans of people observing this image, with remarkable results. A specific region of the cortex, close to the area responsible for the perception of motion, was active when subjects had been viewing the display. Therefore, the effect takes place fairly early on in visual processing, after the image is detected, but just before the higher level cortical processing stages where these images are interpreted in terms of previous learning. However, it is still not fully understood what causes the apparent motion of the spots.

143. What is This?
It is a dancer, whose hands are in the shoes and his head is tucked behind one of his arms. Although all the parts of this image are easily identifiable, they are intentionally posed to present an overall configuration that does not conform to your normal experience. Therefore, your perceptual system, when first presented with this scene, has a hard time grouping the familiar parts into a coherent and meaningful interpretation. After looking at this image for a while, you do some perceptual problem solving so that the overall scene takes on a more meaningful and less bizarre interpretation.

144. A Two Bodied Woman
The head is connected to the body on the right. This illusion takes place because the picture was taken from a very special viewpoint in which only one head is visible and appears to be attached to two different bodies. Human vision usually assumes that we are not seeing objects that are accidentally aligned to produce perceptions that are non-veridical. This assumption is called the 'generic view' principle. Some women seem to do better than men in identifying the correct placement of the head because they use fashion clues. There is no reason, however, to believe that the underlying visual/perceptual system is different between males and females.

145. The Café Escher Illusion
It is not completely understood what causes this illusion, but it is known that it takes place very early on in visual processing, when the brain is encoding edges and contours. The Café Escher illusion is categorized among a class of illusions known as twisted cord illusions.

146. The Presidential Illusion
Look closely at this image and you will see that it is not former President Bill Clinton and Vice President Al Gore. Although Clinton is depicted properly in the foreground, the background figure has Clinton's face, but with Al Gore's hair and trademark black suit. This shows how important context can be in forming your perception of a scene, and how seemingly important details can be inadvertently missed. In addition, hairline and width of the head are important to facial recognition. This illusion works best with people who are quite familiar with the Clinton/Gore team. MIT vision scientist Pahwa Sinha created the Presidential Illusion.

147. Tilted Houses
No, these houses have not collapsed! They are located on a very steep street in San Francisco. The photographer tilted the camera so that it is level with the street, but not with the true horizon, which is obscured. We tend to align the horizontal and vertical with a reference frame. In this case, the frame is furnished by the rectangular shape of the picture, whose horizontal does not correspond to the true horizon line. A horizon line is a very powerful cue for your perceptual system. Therefore, a misleading horizon line, which is not perpendicular to gravity, can produce all sorts of illusions. The woman augments the illusion by leaning in a way that appears to be perpendicular to the street. Ordinarily, she would be perpendicular to the true horizon.

148. Between Illusion and Reality
The physical construction of this scene is impossible. Carefully examine the two passages by first covering the bottom half. You will notice that the top half of the passage extends outward. This is perfectly possible. If you then cover the top half of the passage, you will see that the bottom passage extends inward, which is physically incompatible with the protruding top section. The critical transition occurs at about the upper quarter of the panel with the faint people on the left. That quarter is opaque, but the lower portion appears open. This would almost never occur in natural scenes without a definite boundary between the two.

A drawing, however, is only a suggestion of a three-dimensional scene and by itself is not impossible. It is only your mental reconstruction of it as a real physical object that produces a conceptual paradox. Interestingly, your brain does not reject your paradoxical interpretation. This is because your perceptual system is locked into a series of constraints which dictates how it will interpret a two-dimensional image into a three-dimensional mental representation. This demonstrates that the constraints of your visual system are applied to local portions of the image without global error checking.

149. Floating Vase
Shadows can be a very important cue for your visual system in determining relative height and depth. Normally, shadows are 'attached' to objects which are resting on the ground and not to objects floating above the ground. In this scene, the shadow is not attached to the vase, and therefore the image suggests a floating vase. Specially controlled lighting produced this effect. The image was not digitally altered.

150. Misaligned Eyes
The eyes are perfectly aligned. The circles are a frame of reference for each eye, and your tendency is to judge the alignment in terms of the frames of reference. Since the circles are misaligned, the eyes look misaligned. This illusion only works with a simple two-dimensional representation of a face.

151. Reflectance Illusion
If you look at the region within the dashed rectangle, your visual system cannot determine the physical light sources of the stripes. However, if you cover the right side of the figure and view the left side, it appears that the stripes are due to paint. If you cover the left side and view the right, it appears that the stripes are due to illumination (shading) on the steps. If you view both sides, the percept flip-flops according to where you look.

152. Moretti's Impossible Blocks
Moretti's impossible blocks, aside from their seemingly paradoxical structure, provide another sense of surprise to the viewer. They violate one's expectations about shape constancy, which is the tendency of your perceptual system to keep consistent the true shape of objects, even when they are seen at different orientations. Experience dictates your expectation on how an object should transform as you move around it. If you look at photo A, you see a set of vertically aligned transparent blocks. The lines carefully occlude the structure seen in photo B. We normally don't encounter such 'devious' structures in nature, which is why photos A and B are considered 'non-generic' points of view. Moretti's blocks, because of this occlusion, transform in a very radical way – a vertical alignment transforming to a horizontal alignment.

153. Simultaneous Contrast Illusion
The horizontal gray bar is uniform throughout. The color or brightness of the right side of the bar is contrasted with the light background making it look darker, while the reverse happens with the left side. Current research suggests that this effect is due more to low level contrast mechanisms in vision than to high-level scene interpretation constraints.

154. There's an Angle to This!
In the top photo, although it is hard to believe, all the colored angles are 90° right angles! An image of an angle on the retina is quite ambiguous. We need to know its precise angle in depth. According to Duke University neuroscientists Dale Purves, R Beau Lotto, and Suragit Nundy, the orientation of the angle exerts a strong bias in the judgment of its extent, depending on the frequency of occurrence of particular angles at that orientation in our experience. Angles at the orientation of the red angle tend to be large and that the green angle tend to be small, so we overestimate the red as large and we underestimate the green.

In the bottom photo, although the angles all appear to be identical, they are in fact, quite dissimilar. So, it is quite possible to make physically different angles appear the same by presenting mutually inconsistent information. Although each of these objects appears to form a right angle, none of them project in this way.

155. Filling-in Illusion
Your visual system only responds to the presence of change in a visual scene. This is because a changing stimulus is more important than a static one. Your eyes are constantly making tiny eye movements, which help to keep the visual scene changing and thus visible. The blue dot gradually fades into the green, because there is no reference for the visual system to gauge the eye's movement, and the steady-state stimulus is gradually ignored.

Almost any stimulus that does not change will eventually be ignored, whether it's a tight shoe, an undersized ring or the beating of your own heart. Pain receptors, however, seem to be relatively free of adaptation, which may account for lingering pain.

In addition, a critical factor in this illusion is the fact that human vision tries to spread color to the nearest luminance defined borders. Since there is no strong luminance between the green and the blue, the green spreads out over the blue.

157. Revolving Circles
Although this illusion is not completely understood, it is most likely due to special properties of low level mechanisms for the processing of visual contours. Italian vision scientists B Pinna and G Grelstaff discovered the Revolving Circles illusion in 1999.

159. The Mirror Paradox
The image in the mirror has neither the right nor the left mixed up with the top and the bottom, but the front and the back have been reversed. The problem is on the axis running through the mirror. If you point north then the mirror reflection of you points south. We think of our image as another person. We cannot image ourselves 'squashed' back to front, so we imagine ourselves turned left and right, as if we had walked around a pane of glass to face the other way. It is in this psychological turnabout that left and right are reversed.

So, what about the matchbox experiment? There is no horizontal reversal. But, of course, one sees the back of the match in the mirror. If you painted one side a different color, the color of the mirror image would be different from the direct view.

160. A Taste Illusion
Your sense of smell is really important in discerning the full flavor of foods. This is because receptors in your nose respond to all sorts of molecules that your taste buds do not. So serving gourmet food to someone who has a bad cold is a waste of time.

161. Kitaoka's Spiral
Kitaoka's spiral is a new variation on the classic Fraser Spiral Illusion. It falls into the general category of twisted cord illusions. If you try to trace out the spiral, you will find that it will induce incorrect finger

175 **Angel Glory:** This natural illusion, which is sometimes seen on foggy mountaintops, has been interpreted as an Angel from Heaven; hence its name Angel Glory. A halo also appears around the shadow of your head.

tracing! Even though you conceptually know that this is really a series of concentric circles, your perceptual system will not correct the error. This shows that even your intellect and your knowledge cannot always overcome the constraints of your perceptual system in how you build up a mental image of the outside world.

The illusions 'breaks' when you cover half of the illustration, because your visual system needs to build a 'global' interpretation of the entire image to draw the inference that it is a spiral.

Kitaoka has made a convincing argument that perceived spirals result whenever lines producing tilt illusions in a coherent direction are converted into concentric circles.

164. An Ambulance in an Inside-Out World
The visual system is biased to see convex interpretations rather than concave ones when presented with a stimulus that is ambiguous in this regard. Lighting is critical in making this illusion work, because shape can be determined from shading. This toy ambulance was inspired by a design developed by American magician Jerry Andrus.

166. Breakfast Before and After
Most people spot that the half-eaten doughnut differs from its reflection in the toaster; yet they miss that the level of the coffee in the cup changes. When you look at a scene, your perceptual system tries to ascribe meaning to it based on past experience. However, your perceptual system does not need all the details of an image to do this – only those parts of the image which contribute to the overall meaning of the image. You disregard the rest.

167. Magical Chinese Pool
The paradox with the perceived depth of the pool is a consequence of the refraction of light as it leaves the water which makes the pool's flat bottom appear curved. The base of the pool is light in color so it reflects more light than the upper wall surface, and hence we see the brighter image. It works the same way that a one-way mirror does.

The reason that the cement lines in the pool's wall are straight is because these tiles are not under the water, but are actually the reflection of the wall above the water's surface. These cues also make the pool appear deeper at either end. The pool walls are dark, probably the same color as the wall above, but they are obscured by the reflection of the upper wall. Hence you see the reflected upper wall with straight cement lines, as these lines are not influenced by refraction.

168. Miracle at the Parthenon
The photographer knew that there is no definite location for a rainbow, but only his position relative to the sun and the rain. The photographer positioned himself so that the rainbow would end exactly on the temple.

171. The Magical Mask of Noh
The shape of the mask emphasizes certain features, particularly the contours of the mouth. Slight changes in viewpoint will change the relative position of the corners of the mouth to the lips. Our visual system is particularly sensitive to tiny changes in facial features, and thus interprets the mask as having different emotional expressions.

172. The Mysterious Island and the Magically Appearing Portrait of Jules Verne
Artists have used anamorphic images since the time of Leonardo da Vinci. However, it was Hungarian artist Istvan Orosz who took the art form to a whole new level. Formerly, artists would make a straightforward distortion of an image, which would be revealed on an appropriately placed reflective cylinder. The image by itself would just look distorted. Orosz managed to obscure the image in an overall scene, which could stand on its own without the cylinder.

From a perceptual point of view, this anamorphic print is interesting, because the salient parts of the image are reflected as a meaningful portrait in the cylinder, but the less important and meaningless parts of the landscape do not acquire much significance, and are therefore ignored. This may be due to the fact that recognizing facial expressions and faces are very important for your perceptual system.

173. Brightness Illusion
The black and white checks at the centers of the 'clouds' are identical in brightness to their respective counterpart checks. The 'haze' may be a pictorial cue used to indicate an extreme in luminance. This is a variation on the Kaniza blur brightness illusion.

174. Cross-Modal Illusion
Your perceptual system has evolved a wonderful 'bag of tricks' to resolve the various ambiguities inherent in retinal images. Given an ambiguous stimulus, your visual system will lock onto any reasonable cue that will resolve that ambiguity. In this example, given an ambiguous visual stimulus, a sound can be utilized by your visual system to resolve the ambiguity. However, the sound needs to be made at the point of 'impact'. If the sound comes too early or late, it will not dramatically change your perception.

175. Angel Glory
The Angel Glory, also known as the Specter of the Brocken, is sometimes seen on mountaintops, when you are breaking through the mist with clouds below. The apparition moves as you move and is clearly some magnified projection of yourself. A halo also appears around its head.

GALLERY
VI

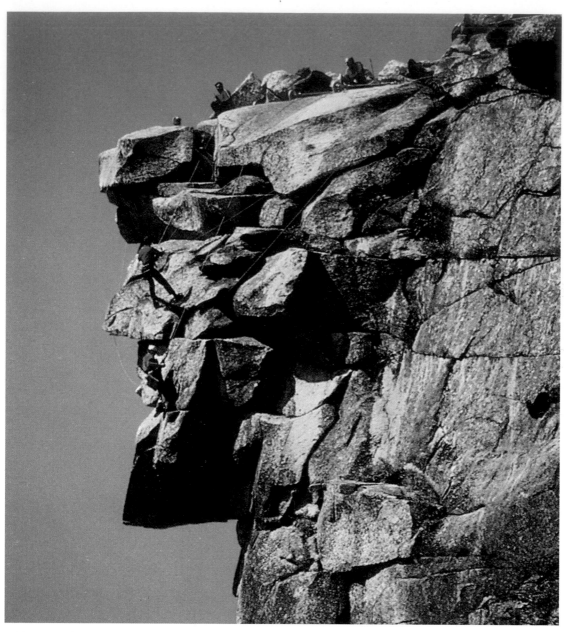

176 **Climbing the Face on the Mountain:** This photograph gives new meaning to the term 'Climbing the face of the mountain'. This rock face is known as 'The Old Man on the Mountain', and is located in New Hampshire, USA.

Previous page: **De Mey's Window:** The little man is contemplating an impossible cube on an impossible windowsill. Belgian artist Jos De Mey created this lovely setting.

177 **Haemaker's Cube:**
Photo A

It is difficult to determine the true shape of this 'impossible cube' sculpture by Belgian artist Matheau Haemaker when seen from only this angle. Compare this view with the adjoining photograph of the same sculpture taken from another angle.

Photo B
What appeared to be straight lines were really curved lines.

178 **An Illusion for the Birds:** On an island off the coast of Maine, in the USA, a puffin, left, stands among three decoy puffins placed there by the National Audubon Society, a conservation group. Because of over hunting, puffins vanished in the 1800s from their island homes. Now people are trying to lure them back. It appears that the decoys are working. So, birds can be fooled too!

179 **An Aqueduct for the Future:** There is something strange about the aqueduct depicted in this scene by Flemish artist Jos De Mey. What is it?

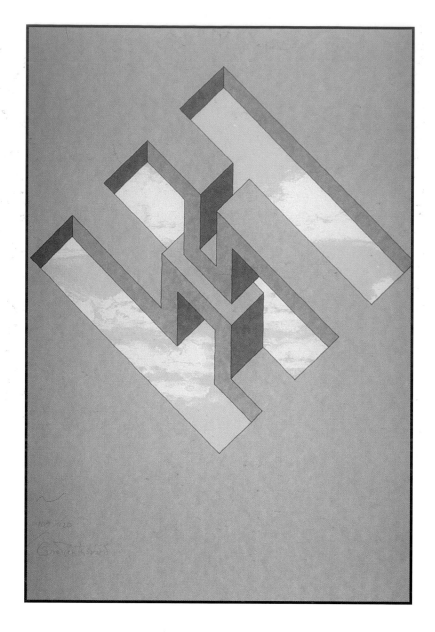

180 A Different Type of Perspective Swiss artist Oscar Reutersvärd confounds us with another one of his impossible illustrations.

181 **Stretched Heads:** The heads on these three figures are strangely distorted. Can you find the angle at which to look at them so that they appear normal?

182 **Anno's Village:** Japanese illustrator Mitsumasa Anno is famous for creating unique worlds. This village can be seen upside down as well as right-side up.

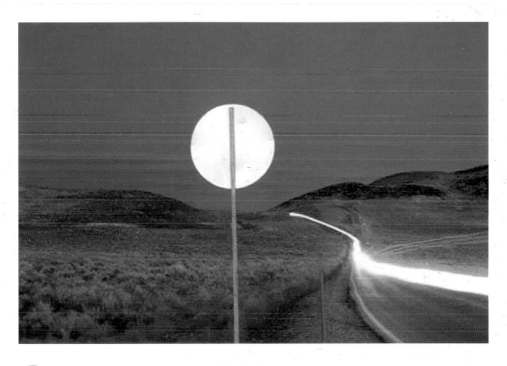

183 **Looking for a Sign of the Moon:** Examine this image. What do you see? Remember that first impressions are not always correct.

184 **Off the Wall:** This woman appears to be leaning off the edge without falling. There are no hidden devices or ropes to hold her up.

185 The Festival of Bacchus:
Look at the three scenes carefully to see how the two people transform into the face of Bacchus.

186 **The Glass Rim Illusion:** Visually estimate, but do not mathematically calculate, the circumference of the glass rim. Would you say that your estimate is less than, equal to, or more than the height of the glass? If you had a piece of string equal in length to the circumference of the rim and put one end at the top of the glass with the rest of it hanging down by the side, how far would it extend?

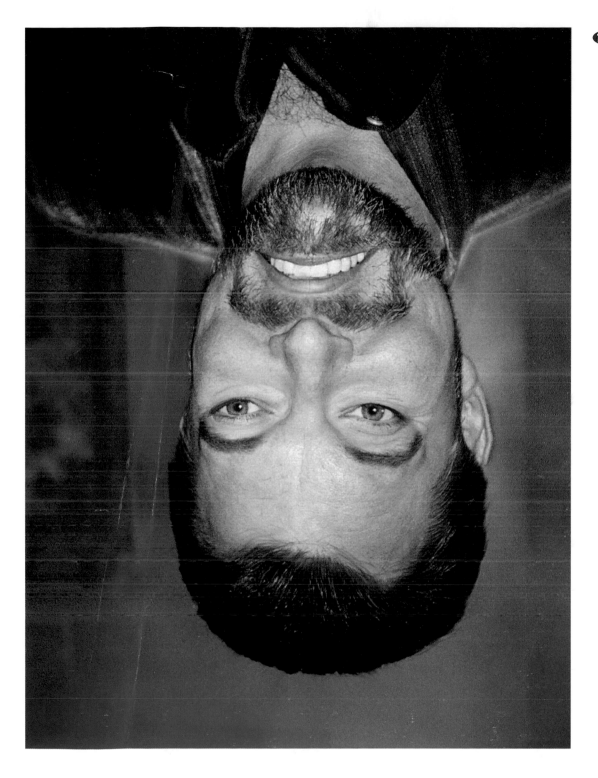

187 The Inverted-Face Illusion: This image of actor Jonathan Frakes does not look too scary, until you turn the picture upside down.

188 **Loch Ness Monster:** Illusions can often be formed by context and expectation. This floating log would never be mistaken for anything but a floating log, except to tourists on Loch Ness. A tourist photographed this log thinking he had captured on film the elusive and famous monster.

189 Impossible Terrace: Are you looking at this structure from above or below? Notice how the ladder also twists in an impossible way. This scene is based on Swiss artist Sandro Del Prete's impossible drawing, 'The Folded Chess Set'.

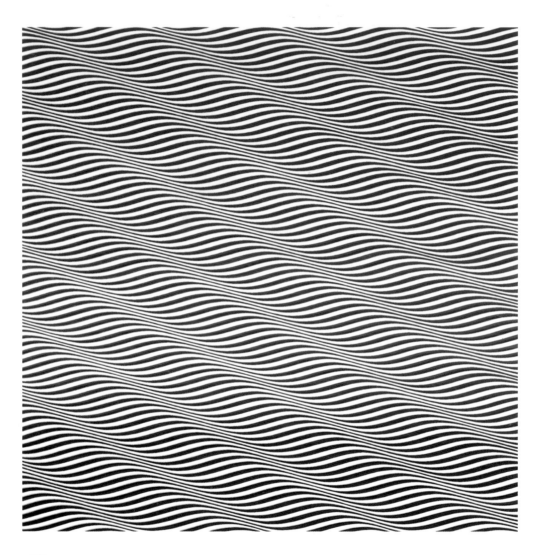

190 **Waves:** Move the picture back and forth and you will see the waves move. American op artist Bridget Riley, who created this image, loved to experiment with images which created the illusion of apparent movement.

191 Eye am a Mouth: The eyes become the mouths in this charming ambiguous drawing by American artist Dick Termes.

192 **A Policeman Looks Surprised:**
Can you make make this policeman look surprised?

193 **An Illusion of Motion:** Japanese artist Shigeo Fukuda depicts the illusion of motion in this beautiful sculpture of a dancer.

Photo A

Compare the two photographs of the same mountain scene. One of these images is the normal photograph, while the other is its negative. Which is which? What clues provide the answer?

Photo B

195 **Square of Three:** *Move this image and it will vibrate and shimmer.*

196 Antisolar Rays: Do the rays of the sun appear to converge at a point just behind the clouds?

197 **Half Faces:** Which face appears happier?

198 A Strange Coincidence: British illustrator Bush Hollyhead captured this bizarre scene at the Fox tavern.

199 Crazy Street: Up and down are perceptually reversed when walking on a crazy street. When you are physically walking downhill, you swear that you are walking uphill and vice versa.

200 Window Gazing: This window is great for looking in two different directions simultaneously! Swiss artist Sandro Del Prete wanted to depict how the world would look if one could look in two different directions at once.

201 **Moon Illusion:** The Moon Illusion is one of nature's most famous illusions. The full moon, just over the horizon, appears to be roughly one and half times the size that it appears to be when it is high over the horizon. The actual angular size of the moon does not change between the two locations.

This doctored picture represents the relative sizes of the horizon and zenith moon, as it would appear to an observer. Interestingly, it is an effect that can't be captured on film. It has to be seen naturally to be appreciated.

202 **Change Blindness:** Compare this photograph with the photograph on the next page, but NOT simultaneously. Flip back and forth between the images to see if you can find the difference.

Photo A

203 **Impossible Triangle to Necker Cube:** These three photographs depict the same bronze sculpture as seen from three distinct views. From one view it looks like an impossible triangle a and from another angle it looks like a wire cube. Look at photograph C to see the intermediary form. Italian artist Guido Moretti created this sculpture.

Photo B

Photo C

204 **A Cat Hidden in its Own Shadow:** Is the black cat walking on a gray pavement or on the grass? Which is the shadow and which is the cat? Rotate the image by ninety degrees in a clockwise direction to be sure.

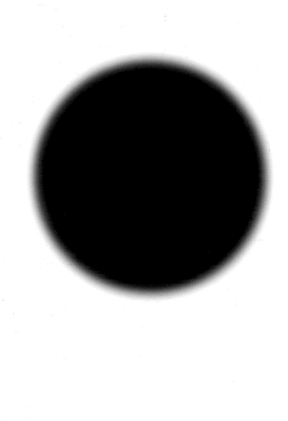

205 **Kanizsa Blur:** Does the right disk appear as dark as the left disk?

206 **School of Fish:** Stare at the fish in this illustration and they will face left and then suddenly change direction and face right.

Notes on Gallery VI

177. Haemaker's Cube
This is another object which violates shape constancy. You have an expectation that this sculpture will transform in a normal way consistent with past experience. This cube is made out of curved sections, which appear straight when viewed from a single point of view. See also the explanation for illusion number 10.

179. An Aqueduct for the Future
The top part of the aqueduct is perpendicular to the bottom part, which would be physically impossible to connect in this fashion.

181. Stretched Heads
Hold the book at waist level and tilt the top part of the page away from you and look along the bottom edge towards the top of the page, so that the image is almost inverted, as seen in the inset. English artist E. Purcell created this anamorphic cartoon in 1822.

183. Looking for a Sign on the Moon
The round disk is not the moon, but the back of a railway sign. Context, not actual features, will mislead most people in this image. Jerry Downs created this contextual illusion.

184. Off the Wall
This is another example of an illusion caused by a misleading horizon line. The woman is really perpendicular to the true horizon, but the true horizon is obscured from the viewer. The room is actually tilted by approximately 26 degrees. The misleading horizon line of the room causes the viewer's internal frame of reference to change and thereby produces the illusion that the woman is leaning and not the room. This orientation illusion can be found in many tourist attractions around the United States.

186. The Glass Rim Illusion
Most people estimate that the circumference around the glass rim is less than the vertical length of the glass. If you measured the rim with a string, and then held it beside the glass it would extend from the top of the glass all the way down to the tabletop, which is consistent with elementary geometry. Try this experiment at home with the cardboard from a toilet paper roll. Which is greater: the circumference of this cylinder, or its height when stood on its end? Cut the toilet paper roll perpendicularly and you'll find the circumference is the longer edge of the resulting rectangle.

In both cases, the illusion is due in part because the lip of the glass is foreshortened and the length of the glass is not foreshortened at all.

187. The Inverted-Face Illusion
We have special areas of our brain devoted to processing faces, including their identity, emotion, gender, and direction of eye gaze. Because our experience with faces is almost exclusively with upright faces, these brain areas have become specialized for processing only upright faces. In particular, we are inefficient at interpreting the emotions of inverted faces. Because the face is initially upside down (only the eyes and the mouth are inverted), this facial area is inactive. When you turn the face right side up, you see the extreme nature of the expression. It has been demonstrated that some species of monkeys, which hang from trees, and routinely see upside down faces, do not have this face inversion effect.

English vision scientist Peter Thompson using a picture of the former English Prime Minister Margaret Thatcher originally created this illusion. Here we carry out the illusion on actor Jonathan Frakes.

190. Waves
The apparent motion here may be produced by contour – activated cells with receptive fields centered at different positions in the visual field – just as occurs with real motion. The undulation may be a consequence of an upper portion of a contour stimulating cells which were previously excited by a lower portion and vice versa.

193. An Illusion of Motion
Japanese artist Shigeo Fukuda used a cultural device to describe 'the illusion of motion'. Most likely you understood what he was trying to depict, because you are used to the popular convention of suggesting movement in static figures by 'motion blurs'. If you look, for example, at static images of automobile advertisements (where the car is ostensibly in motion), you will notice that digital artists have blurred the wheels. This is an artificial convention that we unconsciously accept, but don't actually see in nature. In fact, viewing a photograph of a moving object without a motion blur now looks strange to us. This is an example of a visual cue that has been artificially introduced into our perceptual organization of the world.

194. Negative Mountains
Many people incorrectly believe that the mountain with the snow is the real image. In fact, it is the negative. What people believe is 'snow' is actually the shadows of the mountain. Photo B is the positive. This photo was captured by Jerry Downs.

195. Square of Three
This illusion is similar in effect to number 48 'Waves'.
Many Op artists explored such effects in their works, including the famous painter Bridget Riley. American artist Reginald Neal created this work, which he entitled 'Square of Three'.

196. Antisolar Rays
The sun's rays are actually parallel, but due to perspective effects, they seem to converge.

197. Half Faces
Many people see the right face as happier, even though the faces are mirror-images. The facial expression of the left face has a greater impact on our interpretation of a person's emotion. There is some controversy on whether this asymmetry stems from the fact that the right hemisphere of the brain is more dominant in the processing of facial expressions.

199. Crazy Street
This is another illusion which is caused by a misleading horizon line. The true horizon is kept out of sight from the observer. Normally, the true horizon is perpendicular to gravity, but in this case, vestibular information from your inner ear, which provides us with information about the true direction of gravity, is at odds with your perception of your view of the 'misleading' horizon. This causes an illusion where up and down are somewhat reversed. This is another example of a cross-modal interaction, where one sense influences another.

201. Moon Illusion
The moon illusion has created quite a controversy about what gives rise to the effect, and there are many explanations for why the illusion occurs. The only agreement seems to be that it is not an atmospheric effect.

Part of the complication stems from the fact that there are many visual cues which the brain relies on when assessing size and distance relationships. These cues work fairly well for objects which are relatively nearby, but they tend to break down for objects that are extremely distant, such as the moon, planets, stars, and so forth. Also, the moon illusion is difficult to recreate in an unnatural setting. It does not work at all in a planetarium. Double exposures of the moon taken at both its horizon and zenith positions also destroy the illusion. Separate pictures of both positions also fail to capture the illusion. Therefore, it appears only to work in a natural environment. This is in contrast to many size distance illusions, which can be reproduced photographically or by illustration.

Normally, when objects recede into the distance against a perspective background, not only does their visual angle get smaller, but they also approach a visual horizon. The moon, because of its enormous distance from us, does not change its visual angle much (only about 2 per cent) as it traverses across the heavens. However, your perception of its size does change. This is because your brain is interpreting the image on your retina based on visual cues that it uses for assessing the size and distance of objects in proximity, i.e, between the visual horizon and you.

Also, your visual system tends to be quite good at assessing the size and distance of objects which are resting on the ground, but your visual system has a much harder time assessing the distance of objects that are not 'attached' (floating) with respect to the ground. It is even more difficult for your visual system to assess the proper size and distance of objects if a perspective background has been removed, as in the case with the moon in its zenith position. In fact, there are many other visual cues that are used by the visual system in assessing size and distance relationships, such as ground texture or terrain, angular distance, relative alignment of the object to the true horizon (the moon has no such alignment, being a disk), lens accommodation, surrounding objects, and so forth. These visual cues more or less act in unison, but if they are conflicting with each other, you can get a size distance illusion.

When the moon is on a far horizon, all the intervening details suggests that it is very far away. When the moon is at its zenith position, there are also far less intervening cues available. It is the combination of these factors where your brain is interpreting the same object in a variety of conditions, that gives rise to the moon illusion.

202. Change Blindness
The shadow of the water heater has been digitally removed in the second photograph. This change is difficult to detect because you cannot maintain a detailed memory of either photograph, and must compare items in the two photos individually, or in small groups. In other words, one has to do a systematic visual search pattern to find the change, otherwise you are 'blind' to it.

204. A Cat Hidden in its Own Shadow
The intersection between the gray wall or pavement and the grass is ambiguous, so it is difficult to tell whether the gray area is a vertical wall or pavement. Hence, it is confusing to determine whether the cat's shadow is on the grass or on the wall. However, there are a variety of small cues, such as two ears on the cat, one ear on the shadow, that do give away the fact that the cat is walking on the gray pavement. Joe Burull captured this interesting ambiguous scene.

205. Kanizsa Blur
The right disk does not appear as dark as the left disk, even though they are the same color. The blur of the edges looks brighter (grayer) than the sharp edge, and that edge information is carried across the surface of the disk. Italian vision scientist Gaetano Kanizsa discovered this illusion.

207 **Tessellating Cat, Frog, Dragonfly:** Can you find the dragonfly, cat, and frog in this tessellating pattern by American artist Ken Landry?

GALLERY VII

208 *Sidewinder:* Imagine climbing this set of stairs by Hungarian artist Tomas Farkas. If you start out vertically and walk around, you will end up at the starting point in a horizontal position. Oxford mathematician Roger Penrose came up with a similar design some years earlier.

Previous page: **Two Bodies with One Head:** Which body belongs to the head in this fanciful creation by American artist Dick Termes?

Photo A

This is a three-dimensional sculpture of an impossible rectangle by Belgian artist Matheau Haemaker.

Photo B

When the sculpture is slightly rotated, one can see that it did not transform the way one would have expected. What appeared to be straight edges are actually curved.

Photo C

Here the sculpture is turned at an angle where you can really see its true shape.

210 Numbers Setting 3 Free:
Here the numbers 0–9 are setting the number 3 free. Can you find the numbers 0–9? American artist Jerry Downs created this charming illustration.

211 Strange Scene on an Island Postcard: Spanish surrealist Salvador Dalí created this ambiguous scene after being inspired by a scene on a postcard. Try turning the image by 90 degrees clockwise to see the face.

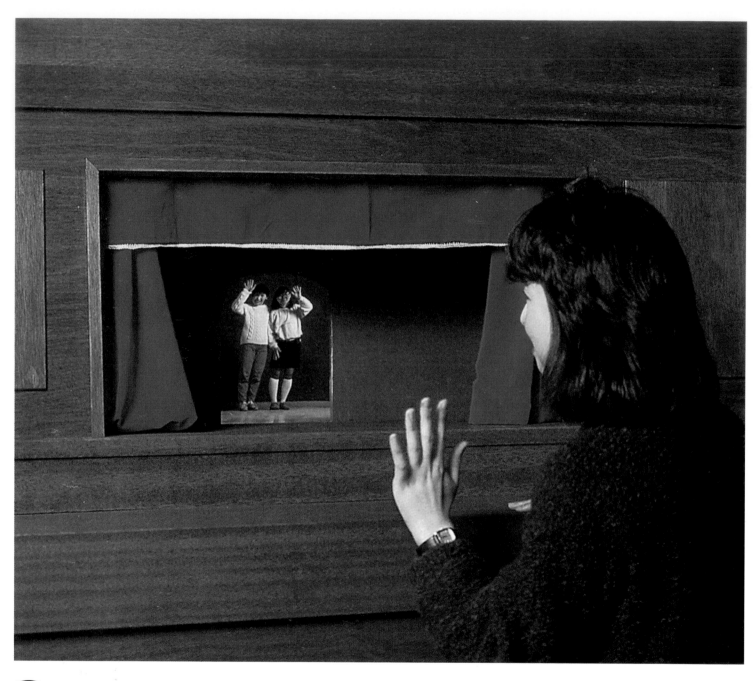

212 **Miniature Theater:** The two girls are life-sized, but they look tiny when seen through the aperture in this miniature theater.

213 **Reutersvärd Triangle with a Twist:** Can you spot the impossibility in this drawing by Swedish artist Oscar Reutersvärd?

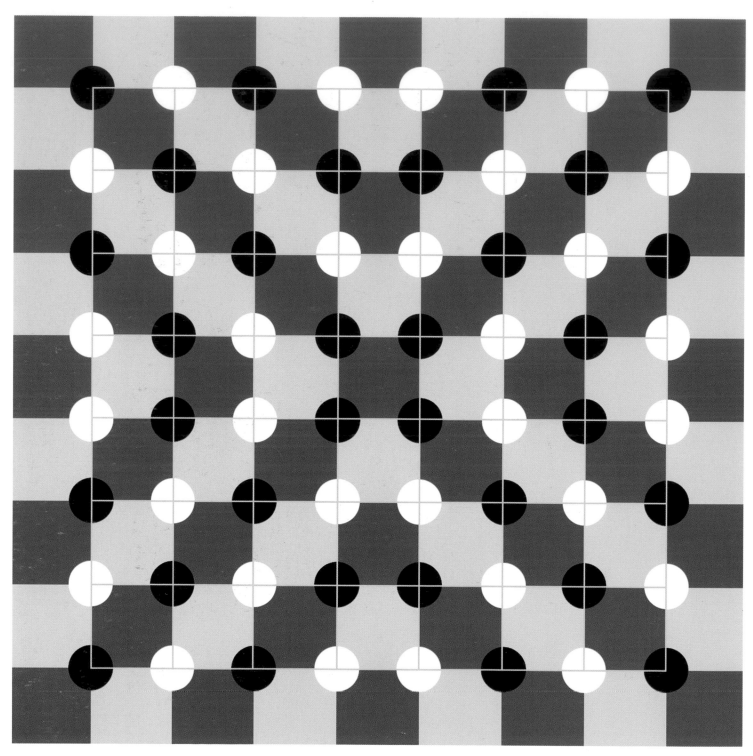

214 **Bulging Lines:** Do the lines appear to be straight or distorted? Check them with a straightedge.

215 Cosmic Wheels: The 'Cosmic Wheels' unleash the powers of the universe in this illustration by Swiss artist Sandro Del Prete.

216 Oops: Oops. . .

217 **Hidden Illusion:** There is an image hidden within the vertical lines. Try moving the image from side to side to see it.

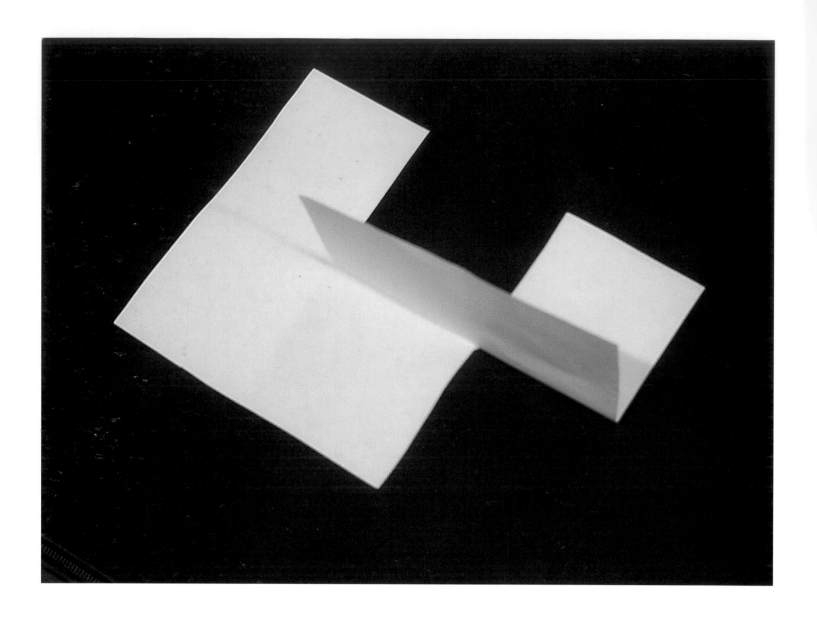

218 **Impossible Fold:** How was this paper folded to create this effect? It appears to be impossible. A rectangular sheet of paper was cut in only two places. No gluing or taping was allowed. See if you can figure it out.

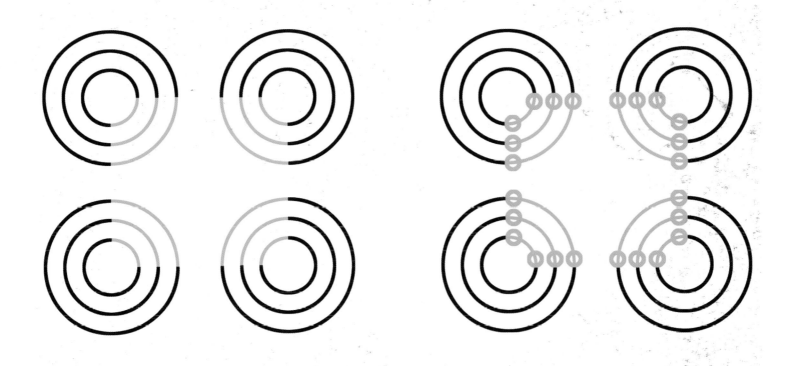

219 Neon Color Spreading: Do the insides of any of the two squares appear to have a slightly bluish tint?

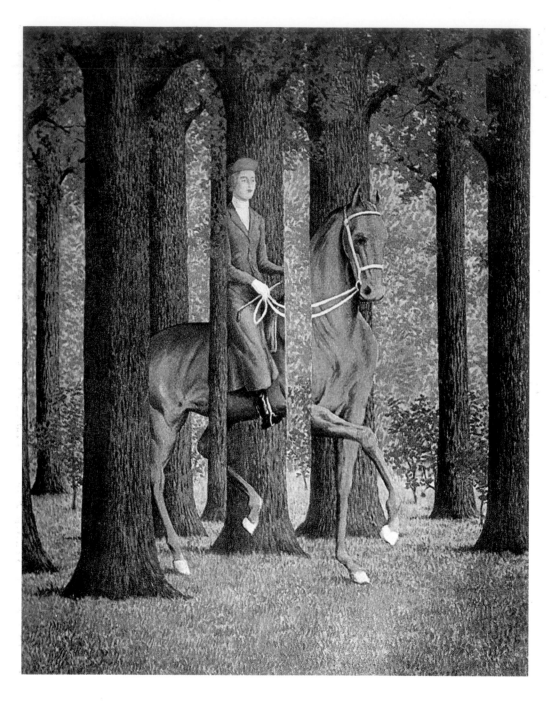

220 **Carte Blanche:** Are the horse and rider on the tree or behind the tree in this painting by René Magritte?

221 **Dali Anamorphosis:** This painting has a blank circle in the middle of it. Only when a cone-shaped mirror is placed on the circle and you look into the point of the cone (as shown) you see a portrait of Dali. Dutch artist Hans Hamngren created this anamorphic homage.

222 **Perceived Gaze Illusion:** *Which Mona Lisa is looking at you? Does the direction of her gaze appear to be different?*

223 **Tiger Photomosaic:** This tiger photomosaic was created entirely out of animal pictures.

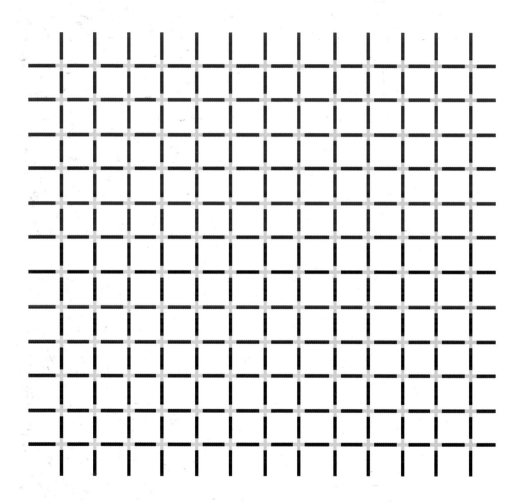

224 **Neon Color Spreading 2:** Do you see bluish disks at the intersections?

225 **Mirror Symmetry of Faces:** One of these faces of Hillary Clinton is distorted. How is it distorted? Taken by itself, does the distorted face look peculiar? This is not meant to be a political satire.

226 Adelson's Mondrian Illusion: The two arrows point to two bands of differing lightness. Does the top band appear darker than the bottom band?

227 **Chevreul Illusion:** Is the contrast of the adjacent rectangles the same throughout? Try covering the border between any two adjacent rectangles with a pencil. What happens?

228 **Soldier of the Lattice Fence:** This warrior is off to fight an impossible battle in this lovely drawing by Swiss artist Sandro Del Prete.

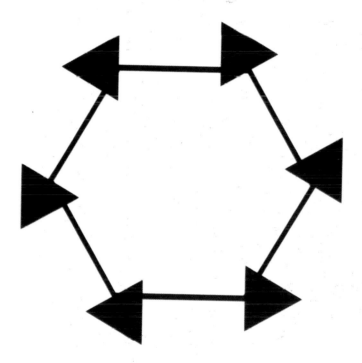

229 **Gerbino's Illusion:** Do the straight-line segments, if connected, appear to form a perfect hexagon?

230 **Hidden Profile of a Queen and her Husband:** Can you find the profiles of Queen Elizabeth II and her husband Prince Phillip?

231 **Borromini's Perspective Arcade:** Why does this man look too large for the corridor?

232 **Domino Face:** American artist Ken Knowlton created this portrait made entirely out of dominoes. The subject in the picture is Joseph Scala, a computer graphics artist and friend of Ken Knowlton. The piece is five feet tall. 'I shot a picture of Joe in his kitchen holding a domino,' Knowlton says. 'I put the photo through one computer program to digitize each tiny area into a shade of gray, then another to establish pairings of cells in the optimal way.' Knowlton used 24 complete sets of double-nine dominos. With 55 in each set, from blank-blank to nine-nine, the piece has 1,320 dominos in all.

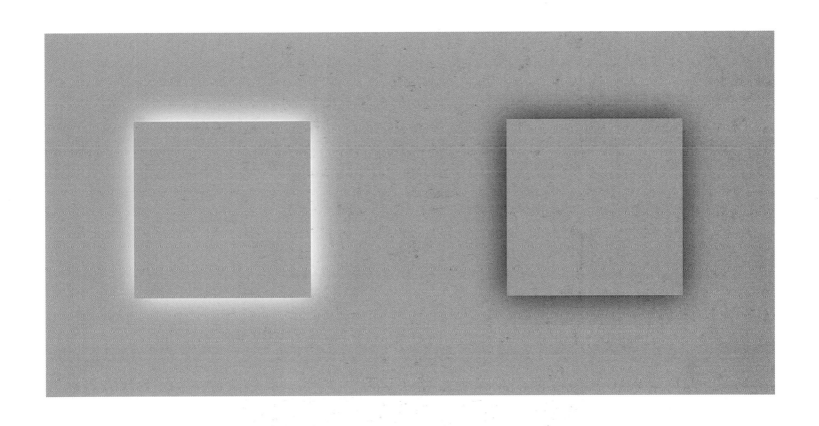

233 Craik-O'Brien-Cornsweet Squares: Do the two gray squares appear to be identical or dissimilar in brightness?

234 Nomad: Note how the two figures transform into the face in this ambiguous illustration by Swiss artist Sandro Del Prete.

235 **The Ganzfeld Effect:** This is a very bizarre experience, which will cause you to have a feeling of blindness. Don't worry, it is completely harmless, and you can stop the effect at will.

You will need a ping pong ball, which is cut in half and a diffused light source, like a fluorescent lamp.

Place the two halves of the ping pong balls over each eye as in the picture. Gaze through them at the fluorescent light for at least five minutes. It is important that you only see diffused contourless light. Do not make any movements which will interfere with your gaze or cast shadows. After a while you will suddenly feel that you cannot see. This feeling of blindness is called 'blank out'.

If someone now casts a shadow over part of your visual field (say a pencil across the path of light), your vision will immediately return with the introduction of this contour!

236 **An Impossibility within an Impossible Triangle:** Swedish artist Oscar Reutersvärd gives us another variation of the impossible triangle.

237 **In or Out:** Do the narrow vertical bands and the broad horizontal bands appear to be raised? Turn the image upside down and how do they appear now?

238 Van Gogh's Sunflowers:
You can see a reflection of Van Gogh's famous Sunflowers in the mirror hanging on the wall. This is a reflection of the distorted three-dimensional anamorphic sculpture lying horizontally before it. Japanese artist Shigeo Fukuda created this anamorphic sculpture.

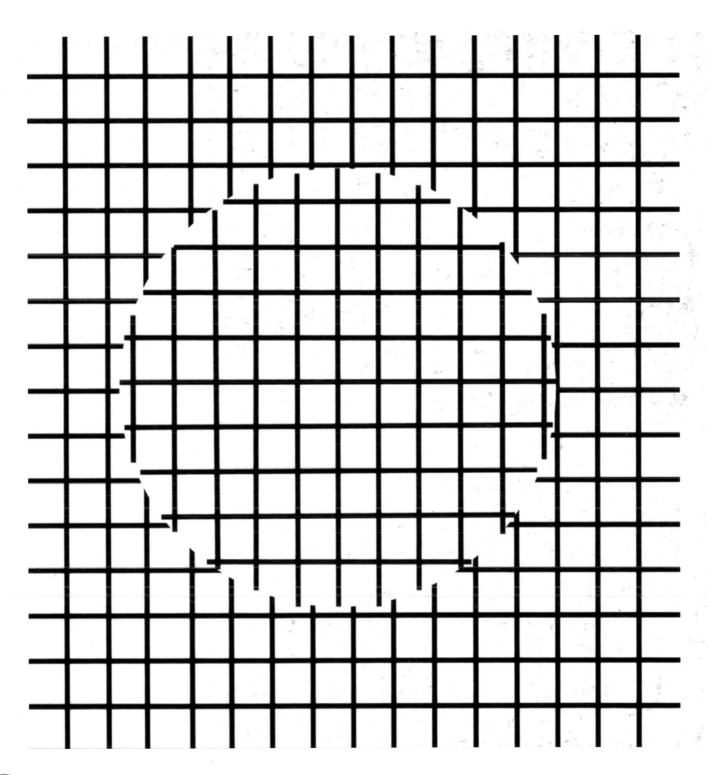

239 **Illusory Circle:** Can you see the illusory circle even though there are no edges or contours to define it?

Notes on Gallery VII

212. Miniature Theater
In assessing size and distance relationships, your brain interprets the images projected onto the back of your retinas. When objects recede into the distance against a normal perspective background, not only does their visual angle get smaller, but they also approach a visual horizon. In the case of the Miniature Theater, the two waving girls are physically far in the distance, so their visual angle is small. The girls' relation to the true horizon is obscured, so that they look tiny when viewed through the aperture. This exhibit is in the famed Deutsches Museum in Germany.

213. Reutersvärd Triangle with a Twist
Look at the top portion of the two bars. One bar passes behind and merges with the other bar in an impossible way. A line normally cannot change its interpretation from convex (as when two surfaces meet away from the viewer) to concave (when two surfaces meet pointing toward the viewer), or vice versa, without passing through a vertex. The upper portion of the lighter colored surface ends in a Y vertex on its right side, with the middle segment being concave. As that segment extends upward toward the red cube it becomes convex without passing through a vertex, clearly an impossibility.

214. Bulging Lines
The lines are all straight. This is another example of a twisted cord illusion by Japanese artist and vision scientist Akiyoshi Kitaoka.

217. Hidden Illusion
It is the figure of a man's face wearing glasses. The lines forming the image are just slightly thicker than the continuation of the rest of the line. This illusion was created by Nicholas Wade.

218. Impossible Fold
This fold is perfectly possible with a rectangular piece of paper. It requires two cuts on either side of the long side of the rectangle about one third of the way down from each side. One side is folded under so that it is now on the opposite side, so you assume that it is the same side as the section of paper at the other end.

219. Neon Color Spreading
The illusory square on the left has a faint bluish color from a phenomenon know as neon-color spreading although the inside of the square is perfectly white. The vertices form the edges of a surface. The visual system tends to spread color within a bounded surface. On the right, when circles are placed at the edges of the illusory square, the neon color disappears. English vision scientist Marc Albert created this demonstration.

222. Perceived Gaze Illusion
There are at least two components to how we determine the direction of gaze. The first is the location of the eye in the eye socket and the second is the direction in which the head is pointed. We normally combine these two sources to determine the direction of gaze. In this case, we have an illusion, because mirroring the image on the right – except for the eyes, which remain unchanged (not reversed) – created the image on the left. This causes a dramatic change in the perceived direction of her gaze. Harvard vision scientist Shinki Ando created this Mona Lisa gaze illusion. W H Wollaston first noticed this effect in 1824.

223. Tiger Photomozaic
The tiger photomozaic was created on a computer with a specialized software program that evaluates the source image, in this case a tiger, in terms of relative values of light, dark, color, edges, and so forth. Once it assigns a numerical value to the source image, it then searches through a database of thousands of images (already stored on the computer) to find the best possible match. The computer will do a pretty good job, but an artist always needs to come in to make it look really good and touch up those areas which the computer missed.

224. Neon Color Spreading 2
The intersections of the black grid are replaced by blue crosses. It looks as if the blue spreads around the crosses and forms blue transparent disks in front of the crossings. A similar illusion without color spreading is also found in Ehrenstein figures. This illusion is associated with color assimilation as well as with illusory contours. In this case, illusory contours are seen based on the color change of the lines, and the color of the lines spreads over the region between the lines. Why does the color spread? This illusion may also be due to the filling in of a uniform surface with a particular color and brightness.

225. Mirror Symmetry of Faces
In the bottom photograph Hillary Clinton's face appears distorted, because her face has been digitally altered to be symmetrical. Most people's faces are slightly asymmetrical. However, it is not true, as maintained in the majority of perception books and articles, that because of this we subconsciously expect people's faces to look symmetrical. If a face is truly symmetrical, and done convincingly by a professional digital artist, a truly symmetrical face does not look strange at all – in fact, just the opposite. It is the sloppiness of the digital artist, as in this example, that gives rise to the perception that the face is distorted, not the fact that the face is symmetrical.

226. Adelson's Mondrian Illusion
The gray stripes are identical. MIT vision scientist Ted Adelson modified the standard simultaneous contrast illusion with the addition of transparent horizontal stripes, which augment the illusion.

227. Chevreul Illusion
When you place a pencil over the borders between any two adjacent rectangles, the two rectangles appear identical. in brightness. Yet, they are not identical. We are primarily sensitive to sharp differences in brightness, as exists at the borders between the rectangles. When these are covered, all that remains is a slight gradient, to which we are largely insensitive. This is known as Chevreul's Illusion.

229. Gerbino's Illusion
The lines, if connected, would form a perfect hexagon. The points where they would connect are 'masked' by the triangles. The visual system tends to continue lines when they disappear behind an occluding object, as they do in this case. The end point of each segment appears to be near the center of each triangle, which causes the perception of misalignment. Italian vision scientist Walter Gerbino created this illusion.

230. Hidden Profile of a Queen and her Husband
This vase is based on the famous two-dimensional figure ground illusion of Danish psychologist Edgar Rubin. This goblet, based on Rubin's concept, was made as a gift for the silver jubilee anniversary of Queen Elizabeth II and her husband, Prince Philip. If you view the dark area as the figure, instead of the ground, you will see the outlines of the two profiles (facing each other) on either side of the goblet. The Queen and her husband were delighted with the gift.

231. Borromini's Perspective Arcade
This illusion arcade, which can be found in the inner courtyard of Palazzo Spada, Rome, gives a false impression of depth. The columns literally get smaller the farther back they go, as do the ceiling coffers; the floor slopes upwards, and the cornices downwards; the columns are thicker at the front than the back; and the 'squares' on the pavement are actually trapezoids. Francesco Borromini, one of the most important architects of the 1600s, created it.

233. Craik-O'Brien-Cornsweet Squares
This variation on the simultaneous contrast illusion shows that a small border is enough to make the two identical gray squares look different in lightness. This is known as the Craik O'Brien Cornsweet illusion.

235. The Ganzfeld Effect
Contours are the basic building blocks of visual perception; in their absence we actually lose our ability to see. This Ganzfeld demonstration eliminates contours in your visual field, so vision fails. When a contour, or any luminance change, is perceived, vision immediately returns. A blank out can also occur in natural environments. Snow blindness is a kind of natural blank out, caused by the lack of contour in the retinal image when the visual field contains a lot of snow and ice. The snow and ice scatter much of the light in all directions, and together are very uniform in texture, which creates a natural Ganzfeld effect.

237. In or Out
This is a shape from shading illusion. Normally, light comes from above, and the shadows in the first alignment are consistent with this interpretation. When you turn the image upside down, the visual system is guided by the same constraints about the direction of light, so it now assumes that the bands are depressed rather than raised. However, both interpretations are somewhat ambiguous, and it is possible to see either orientation as either raised or depressed.

239. Illusory Circle
This is known as a subjective contour, because the contours of the circle are not physically present. The construction of these contours requires sophisticated non-local (neurons from a substantial area of the brain) processing in the brain.

240 Dali's Anamorphosis:

Photo A

Spanish surrealist painter Salvador Dalí also created anamorphic images. Compare this image with the adjoining image to see what is revealed in the reflective cylinder.

Photo B

The picture above has been turned upside down and a reflecting cylinder added. Do you see the knight and his horse in the reflection?

GALLERY VIII

241 **Legs of two different Genders:** *Are these men's legs or women's legs? This illustration is by Japanese artist Shigeo Fukuda.*

Previous page: **Flip-Flop:** *Are the red surfaces facing up or down? Keep looking: they will appear to flip to face the other direction due to contradictory depth cues. This ambiguous figure was provided by American artist Joan Miller.*

242 **Romeo and Juliet:** In this drawing, Swiss artist Sandro Del Prete symbolically depicts the impossible barriers of love between Romeo and Juliet.

243 **Tessellating Escher:** This image contains multiple tessellating portraits of Dutch graphic artist M.C. Escher. Escher was famous for creating tessellating images. Turn the picture upside down and it still works. American artist Ken Landry created this tessellating topsy-turvy homage to Escher.

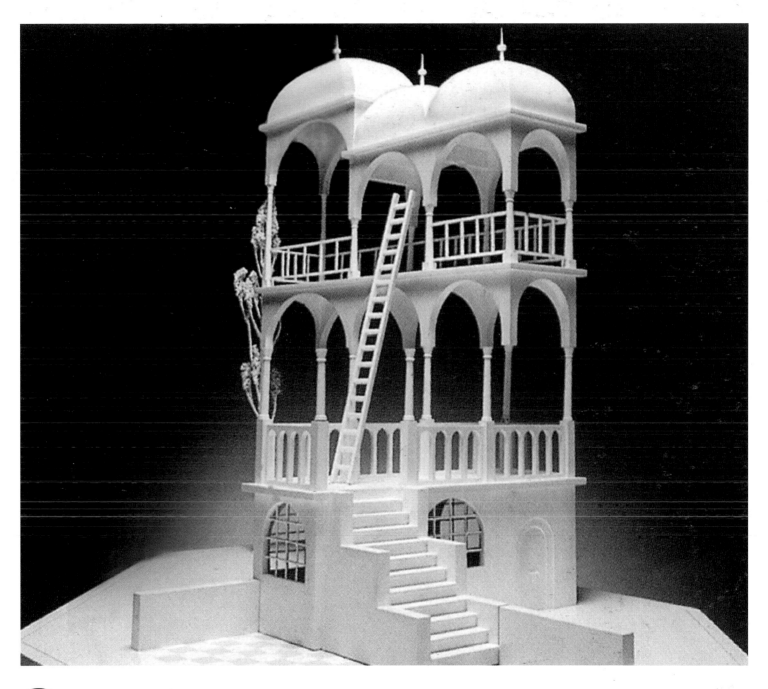

244 **Belvedere:** This is a physical model of an impossible building, based on the structure depicted in M.C. Escher's famous print, 'Belvedere'. The top floor is perpendicular to the bottom floor, yet they are perfectly joined. The ladder is also in a peculiar position. Japanese artist Shigeo Fukuda made this physical model.

245 **Beckoning Balusters:** Can you find the figures hiding in between the columns?

246 **Shape from Shading:** The top and bottom halves of this figure look like they are curving outward or inward, depending on whether you think the light comes from the left or right side. Try to imagine a light shining from the left – the top half will appear to curve out and the bottom half will appear to curve in. If you imagine the light as coming from the right side, then the top half looks like it curves inward.

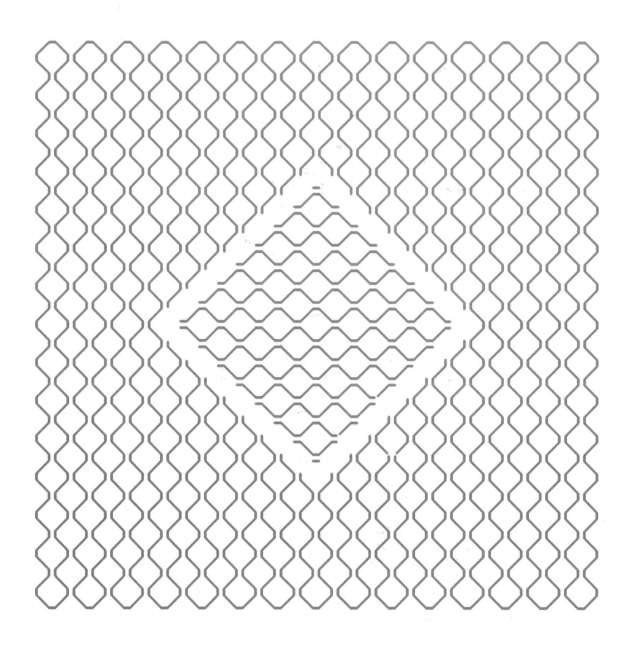

247 **A UFO Caught in a Mesh:** Move this illustration from side to side and you will see the center section move separately from the surrounding section.

248 Afterimage: Stare at this image for thirty seconds or more without averting your eyes or attention. Then quickly look at a blank sheet of paper. You will see a glowing afterimage.

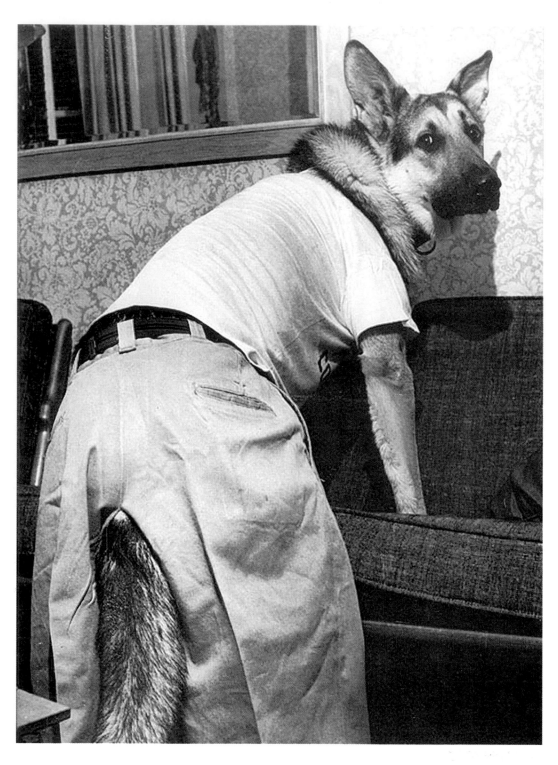

249 More and More Human: *What's going on here? Take a close look.*

250 **Hidden Tools:** How many tools can you find?

251 **A Twist on Reginald Neal's 'Square of Three':** The three blue squares in the center appear to be tilted with respect to one another when placed against the background of Reginald Neal's famous painting 'Square of Three'.

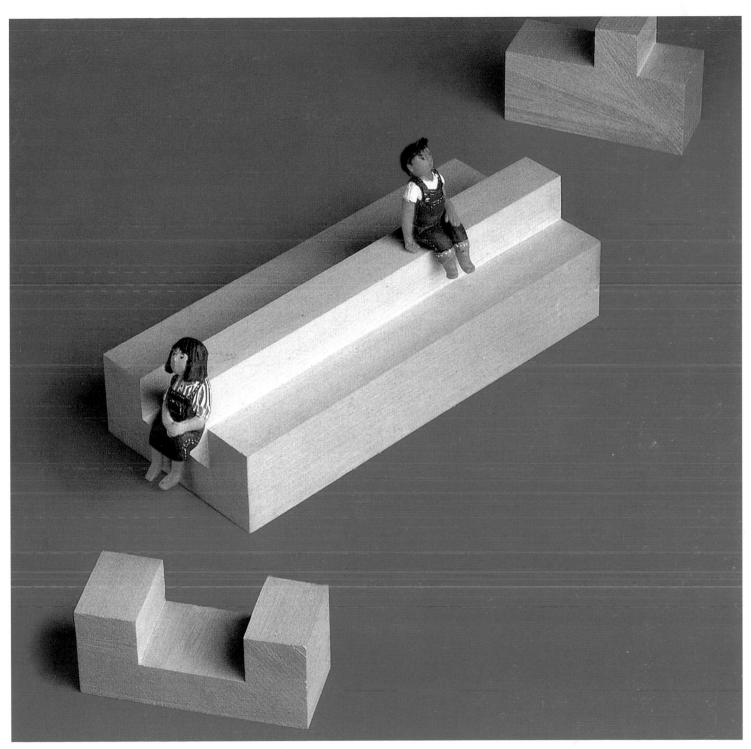

252 **Nob's Impossible Ledge:** The plastic figure on the right is sitting on top of a wooden step, which corresponds to the piece separated on the right. If you follow the ledge to the left, you will see the other plastic figure sitting in a carved out depression, which corresponds to the separated piece on the left. How could this be possible?

253 **Assimilation Illusion:** Does the gray center square appear darker than the gray that surrounds it?

254 Can You Spot the Difference?: Are the five gray and white blocks all identical in color and brightness? Does a gray block appear to rest upon a lighter block in the prominent set of blocks in the foreground?

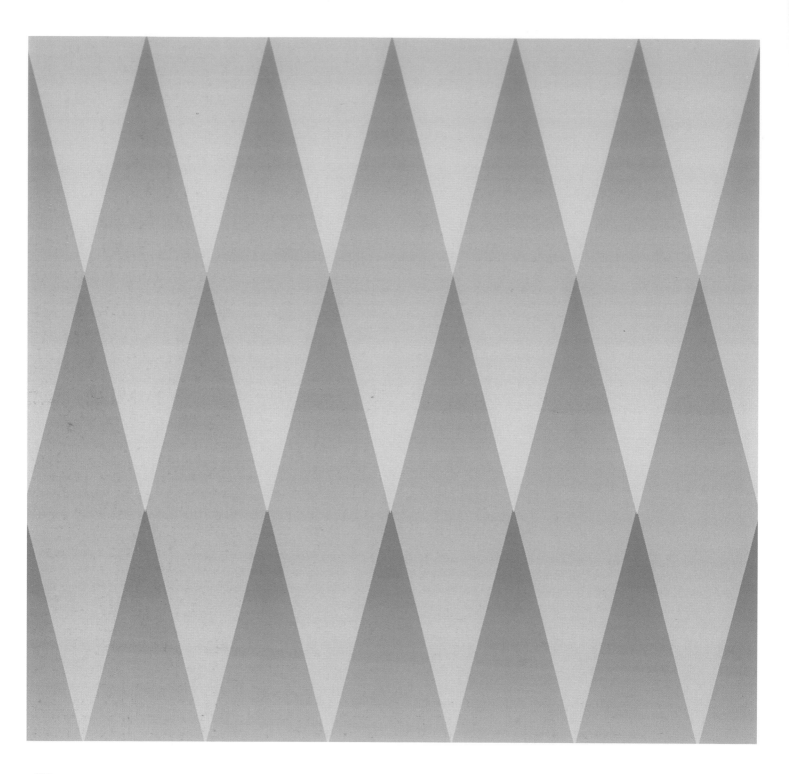

255 **Diamond Illusion:** Here are two rows of complete diamond shapes. Which row is darker – the bottom row or the top row?

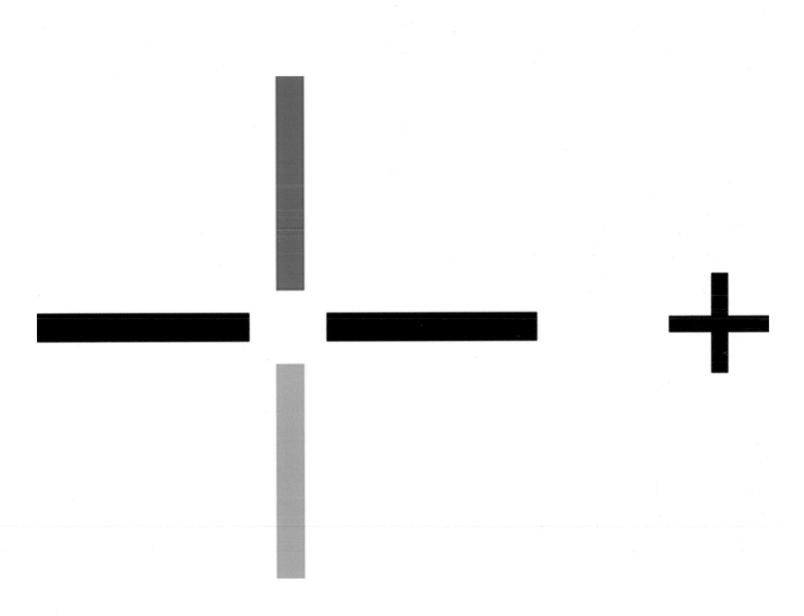

256 **Color Blind Spot Illusion:** This is a blind spot illusion. Find your blind spot by closing your right eye while simultaneously looking at the small black cross with your left eye. Move the image nearer until the center blank square in the left figure falls in your blind spot. The formerly blank area will be filled-in. What color is the vertical arm over this area? Is it red? Is it green? Is it some other color?

257 **Outline Can Determine Shape:** The figures depicted here appear to have three very different three-dimensional shapes, although their shading is identical. The only difference is the outline of the different shapes.

258 **Rubik's Cube Illusion:** Does the 'brown' square in the top of the Rubik's cube appear to be identical in color with the 'yellow' square that is in the middle of the side? They sure don't appear to be identical in color, yet haven't we fooled you so far?

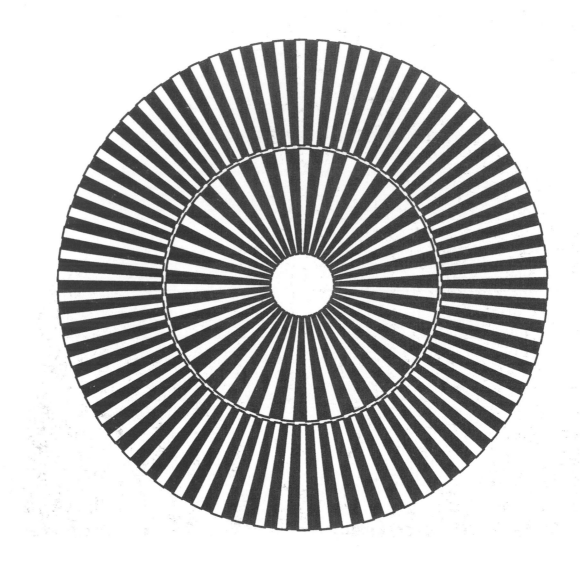

259 **The Hula-Hoop Illusion:** View this figure while giving the page a wide circular movement, but do not change the figure's orientation.

260 **Stone Windows:** A typical building in New York City, or is it? Perhaps if you compare the larger photo with the photo inset, you will notice that one side of the building is almost entirely painted. The artist is Richard Haas and he entitled this work '112 Prince Street Facade'. Note the painted side includes open windows, pulled shades, and air conditioners (with shadows). This form of artwork is known as trompe l'oeil.

261 **Impossible Staircase:** This is a physical model of an impossible staircase. Can you find either the bottom or top stair? To see how the model was made look at the bottom photograph.

Photo A

Photo B

262 **Colored Diamonds:** *Are the diamonds all identical in their shade of green?*

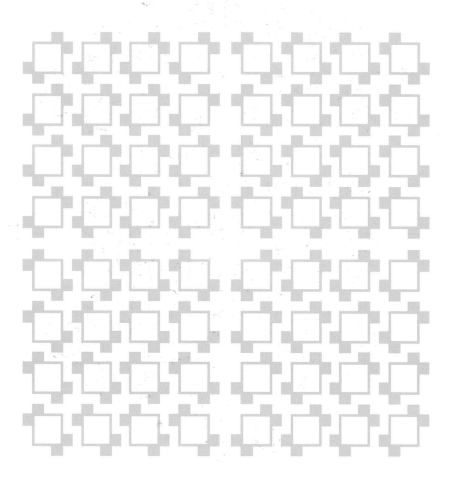

263 **Exploding Squares:** Do the squares appear to be exploding?

264 **A King and His Queen:** This gruff, bearded king, drawn by artist Rex Whistler, is frowning because he can't seem to find his queen. He is ready to turn his whole kingdom upside down to find her. Do you think he will be successful? Can you find her?

265 Anamorphic Stairs: From one angle, the figure on the stairs appears perfectly normal, but when you see the same figure from a different angle, it appears quite distorted.

266 **Tilt Induction Effect:** Do the vertical bars appear to be tilted?

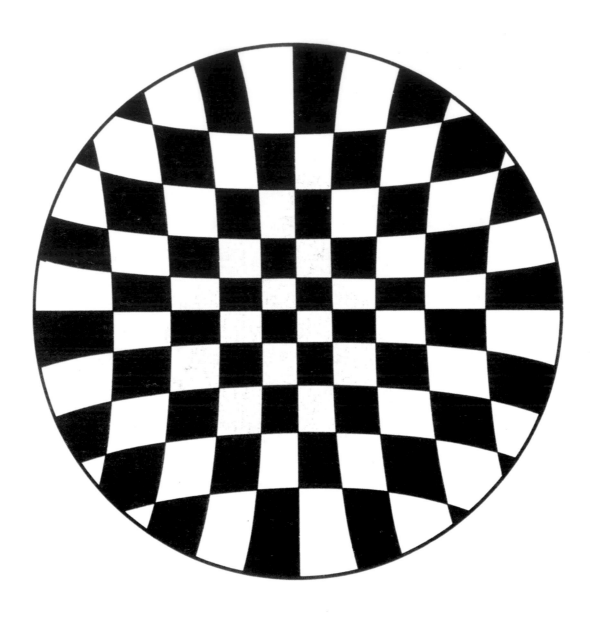

267 **Fisheye Illusion:** Using only one eye, bring the image within 3 cm of your eye. Do the curved lines now look straight?

268 **Bottom's Up:** Where is the bottom and top of the hole that the figures are sitting upon?

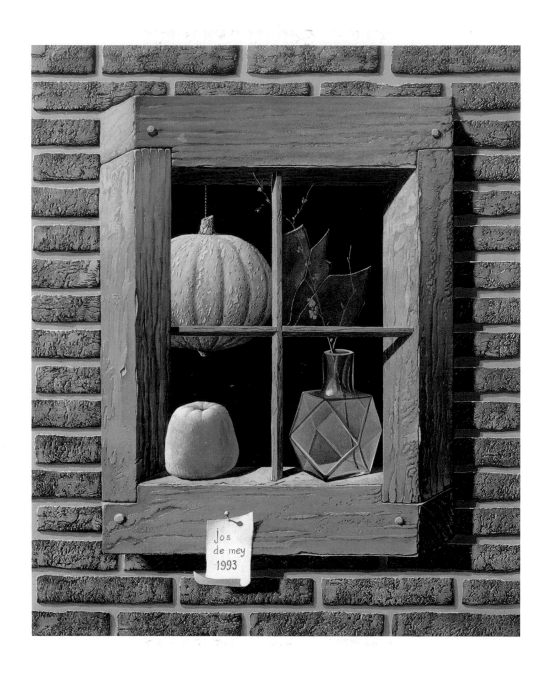

269 **Still Life in an Impossible Windowsill:** Flemish artist Jos De Mey captured this still life in his windowsill. How can this be?

270 **Bezold Effect:** Compare the red horizontal lines in both figures. Do they appear to be an identical shade of red?

271 **Color Assimilation:** Do you perceive a reddish hue within the white squares on the right and a bluish hue within the white squares on the left?

272 **Reflections of an Impossible Object:** The reflection of this object in the mirror looks like an impossible rectangle, but its true form can be seen in front of the mirror.

Notes on Gallery VIII

245. Beckoning Balusters
The standing figures are found in between the columns. The outlines of the opposing columns form their outline.

246. Shape from Shading
Your brain uses clues to determine depth from a two-dimensional picture. One clue is shading. In this illusion the shading is ambiguous. Thus, depending upon where your brain perceives the light is coming from, the shading will dictate whether the bulges are perceived as convex or concave.

247. A UFO Caught in a Mesh
Japanese vision scientist Akiyoshi Kitaoka created this variation of the Ouchi apparent motion illusion. The intersections between the vertical texture and the horizontal texture seem to trigger your visual system's motion detectors in different ways. When the page is moved back and forth you will perceive illusory motion in depth.

248. Afterimage
When you focus on the woman's face, light-sensitive photoreceptors (whose job it is to convert light into electrical activity) in your retina respond to the incoming light. Other neurons that receive input from these photoreceptors respond as well. As you continue to stare at the face your photoreceptors become desensitized. Your photopigment is 'bleached' by this constant stimulation. The desensitization is strongest for cells viewing the brightest part of the figure, but weaker for cells viewing the darkest part of the figure. When you quickly look at a white sheet, the least depleted cells respond more strongly than their neighbors, producing the brightest part of the afterimage: the glowing face. This is a negative afterimage, in which bright areas of the figure turn dark and vice versa. Positive afterimages also exist. Most afterimages last only a few seconds to a minute, since in the absence of strong stimulation, most nerve cells quickly readjust.

Afterimages are constantly with us. When we view a bright flash of light, briefly look at the sun, or are blinded by the headlights of an approaching car at night, we see both positive and negative afterimages.

251. A Twist on Reginald Neal's 'Square of Three'
Radiating lines and other such geometrical background configurations can distort one's perception of lines and shapes. In this case, the three perfect squares appear to be distorted when placed against such a background. This illusion belongs to a class of illusions known as angle-expansion illusions. It is not perfectly understood what causes this illusion.

252. Nob's Impossible Ledge
This wooden model, created by Japanese puzzle inventor Nob Yoshigahara, is impossible only from this one viewpoint. This time we won't reveal the solution. We want you to think about it.

253. Assimilation Illusion
The gray in the middle box and the surrounding gray are identical. A gray background crossed by fine dark lines produces a darker gray. Conversely, the fine white lines will pull the value of the gray background toward the white. This is an assimilation illusion.

254. Can You Spot the Difference?
The blocks are not all identical in color, although they appear to be. The set of blocks in the far-left background and the prominent set of blocks in the foreground are identical with each other, but not identical with the remaining blocks. Cover the middle portion of the prominent middle set of blocks. You will see that although it appears to be a darker block resting on top of a lighter block, both blocks are identical. This is true also of the set of blocks in the far-left background. The other blocks, however, are made out of a gray

block and a lighter block. So in this image, there is a set of blocks that fools you, and a set of blocks that does not fool you, yet the dissimilar sets of blocks give rise to the very same perception! This scene combines perspective, orientation, texture, additional gradients and objects, and a distinctive background (the areas surrounding the two surfaces, i.e., the sky and ground, have the same average luminance), in such a way that suggests that the two equiluminant blocks (the object in the foreground) have a high probability of being differently reflective surfaces in light and shadow respectively. Thus, reality doesn't matter to the visual system, it insists that the blocks 'must' be two different shades, even though they are not. Duke neuroscientists Dale Purves and R. Beau Lotto created this wonderful enhanced demonstration of the Cornsweet illusion.

255. Diamond Illusion
The bottom row of diamonds is identical with the middle row of diamonds. This is a variation on the Craik O'Brien Cornsweet simultaneous contrast illusion where a small border is enough to make the two identical pink diamonds look different in lightness.

256. Color Blind Spot Illusion
The blind spot is an area of the retina where the nerves and blood cells of the eye pass through. Because there are no photoreceptors there, the brain fills in the gap with its best guess so that you don't notice that part of the world that you are looking at is missing.

257. Outline Can Determine Shape
Vision scientists have repeatedly shown how shading can dramatically influence your perception of a figure's three-dimensional shape. In this case, Japanese vision scientist Isao Watanabe demonstrates how three figures can have identical shading, yet suggest three very different and distinct three-dimensional shapes. The only difference is their outlines.

258. Rubik's Cube Illusion
Unbelievable as it seems, the 'brown' square on the top of the Rubik's cube is identical in color with the 'yellow' square that is in the middle of the cube's side. You can test this by covering everything except those two squares, and then when compared, you will see that they are identical. Duke University neuroscientists Dale Purves and R. Beau Lotto have used this new illusion to show dramatically that color perception is based on past experience. The block image illustrates how changing the empirical meaning of a scene – in this case removing the confounding shadows – not only changes the brightness that people perceive, but also the colors.

259. The Hula-Hoop Illusion
View this figure while giving the page a wide circular movement, but do not change the figure's orientation. You should see the two circles move at differently perceived rates. Vision scientist Nicholas Wade first described the 'Hula-Hoop' illusion.

262. Colored Diamonds
All the diamonds are identical in their shade of green. This illusion is similar to illusion number 119.

263. Exploding Squares
The 'illusion of the flying squares' is created by attaching black squares in a special configuration that makes a three-dimensional impression. Every figure consists of squares and every angle is a right angle. There are no curves. The illusion is an orientation illusion specific to corner squares. The specific placement of the little dark squares around the edges of the larger white square causes your perception of the white square's border to be contracted. Japanese vision scientist Akiyoshi Kitaoka created this illusion.

264. A King and His Queen
To find the Queen, turn the image upside down. Rex Whistler, an English muralist who died in 1944, left behind a wonderful set of upside down portraits. In 1946, a London publisher posthumously published 15 of these topsy-turvy portraits in an invertible book appropriately entitled, OHO.

265. Anamorphic Stairs
Hungarian artist Istvan Orosz created this anamorphic figure of a person climbing a set of stairs. In a normal painting of a figure, the image does not appear to distort as you walk past it. In this anamorphic image, the viewing point is absolutely critical, and the image distorts as you walk by.

266. Tilt Induction Effect
Although the vertical bars appear to be tilted outwards, they are not. This is known as a tilt induction effect, where the vertical line appears slanted in the direction opposite to the context lines. This illusion is thought to have some relationship to the classic Zöllner illusion. The tilt induction effect is greater when the context lines are near vertical than when they are near horizontal. In the tilt induction effect, visual cues (the oblique lines) cause errors in the perception of orientation, owing to mistakes in judging visual context.

267. Fisheye Illusion
The curvature of the back of your retina introduces a distortion in the way you perceive the lines. You rarely, if ever, notice this distortion, because you normally do not use only one eye, where the image covers most of the retina.

270. Bezold Effect
The red horizontal lines are identical in both figures. This is known as the Bezold effect, where context can influence your perception of a surrounding color. In the Bezold effect, colors will appear to expand beyond their borders and mix with neighboring colors. It is the reverse of the much more familiar effect of simultaneous contrast in which a color tends to induce its opposite in hue, value and intensity upon an adjacent color. Viewing distance and angle change the appearance of colors and the pictorial structures. Look at the image with your eyes squinted: this may enhance the effect. The colors in two identical pictures appear to be different when one of them is turned by 90° and compared to the other.

271. Color Assimilation
The white squares on the red background look reddish, and those on the blue background look bluish. Thus, the white squares take on their background's colors. Such a phenomenon is called color assimilation. This is the opposite of color contrast. The contrast and assimilation phenomena are also found for brightness and darkness. While the physiological mechanisms for brightness and color contrast phenomena are well understood, how and when the assimilation occurs are not.

272. Reflections of an Impossible Object
This physical model of an impossible rectangle only works from one special angle. Its true construction is revealed in the mirror. Even when presented with the correct construction of the rectangle (as seen in the mirror), you brain will not reject its seemingly impossible construction (seen outside the mirror). This illustrates that there is a split between your conception of something and your perception of something. Your conception is ok, but your perception is fooled. Bruno Ernst constructed this physical model.

Glossary

Accommodation
Accommodation is the process by which the lens of the eye varies its focus when looking at objects of differing distances. Accommodation may serve as a weak depth cue over short distances.

Afterimage
An Afterimage is the visual persistence of a retinal image after the stimulus is gone. It is due to either intense or prolonged stimulation with constant eye fixation. Most people are used to the experience of afterimages after briefly staring at the sun or a bright light source, and seeing the resulting afterimage, which eventually fades out. Both positive and negative afterimages exist.

Ambiguous Figure
Ambiguous figures are single images which can give rise to two or more distinct perceptual interpretations. Most people find that one interpretation can switch to another readily, but they never can see both interpretations at once. It is common for the percepts to flip-flop, depending on various factors.

Anamorphic Image
Anamorphic images are drawings which have been stretched or distorted in a way so that their 'normal' configuration is revealed only on a reflected surface or from a particular critical viewing angle.

Attention
Attention is the concentration on a particular stimulus, sensation, or thought while excluding others. Attention is a broad term that probably covers more than one type of brain mechanism.

Blind spot
The blind spot is a region of the retina in which there are no receptors because the axons of ganglion cells exit the eye and pass into the optic nerve. Therefore this is an area without photoreceptors and hence this region shows no response to light.

Brightness
Brightness is the perceived intensity of light coming from the image itself, rather than any property of the portrayed scene. Brightness is sometimes defined as perceived luminance.

Cones
Cones are short, thick, tapering nerve cells in the photoreceptive layer of the retina which are specialized for bright-light and color vision. There are three types of cone-shaped photoreceptors that are responsible for the perception of color. Cones are heavily concentrated in the center of the retina (the fovea), but some are found throughout the periphery.

Contour
A contour is any place in the retinal image where the light intensity changes abruptly. It is the boundary of a region. Normally it is an edge that is assigned to the region of one side or the other, depending upon several factors influencing figure/ground organization.

Contrast
The contrast between two adjacent regions is their relative luminance levels.

Cues
Cues are features of visual stimuli which prompt the perception of depth or vision.

Filling-in
Filling-in is an action by the brain which 'guesses' the nature of absent information by assuming that it resembles related information.

Figure
Figure refers to an image region to which its contours have been assigned, producing the perception of being a perceptual element whose shape is defined by the contour and that 'stands out' in the center of attention.

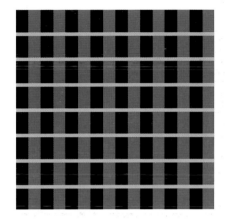

Global
Global refers to the overall arrangement of parts of a figure, as opposed to the local details or parts that make up the overall figure.

Ground
Ground refers to regions to which contours have not been assigned (see *Figure*), producing the perception of being in the background and extending behind the figure.

Illusory Contours (or Subjective Contours)
Illusory contours are visual experiences of edges where no corresponding physical luminance edges are present in the image.

Impossible Figure
Impossible figures are two-dimensional line drawings which initially suggest the perception of a coherent three-dimensional object that is physically impossible to construct in a straightforward way.

Impossible Object
Impossible objects are physical objects, as opposed to two-dimensional drawings, that suggest an impossible construction. These objects usually require a specialized viewing angle to see the paradox.

Lateral Inhibition
Lateral inhibition is the process of adjacent neurons inhibiting one another.

Lens Accommodation
See *Accommodation*.

Lightness
Lightness is the perceived reflectance of a surface. It represents the visual system's attempt to extract reflectance based on the luminances in the scene.

Luminance
Luminance is the amount of visible light which comes to the eye from a surface.

Optic Nerve
The optic nerve is the collection of axons from retinal ganglion cells as they exit the eye.

Perception
Perception is the conscious experience of objects and object relationships.

Orientation
Orientation is the property of objects concerning their alignment with respect to some reference line, such as gravity or the medial axis of the head.

Reflectance
Reflectance is the proportion of incident light that is reflected from a surface.

Retina
The retina is the curved surface at the back of the eye that is densely covered with over 100 million light sensitive photoreceptors plus other sensory neurons (amacrine, bipolar, ganglion, and horizontal cells) which process the output of the receptors. Curiously enough, the photoreceptors are situated in the innermost layer while the ganglion cells, whose axons project to the brain, lie in the outermost layer, nearer to the lens of the eye. For this reason there has to be a gap in the retina through which the axons of ganglion cells can pass on their way to the brain. This gap in the photoreceptor layer produces a blind spot in each eye.

Retinal Image
The retinal image is the two-dimensional distribution of light of various intensities and wavelengths on the retina.

Rods
Rods are long, thin, cylindrical photoreceptors in the retina, used exclusively for vision at low levels of illumination. Rods are extremely sensitive to light and are located everywhere in the retina except at its very center (fovea).

Salient
An object is said to be salient if it attracts attention; stands out conspicuously

Sensation
Sensation is the simple conscious experience associated with a stimulus.

Shape Constancy
Shape constancy is the process by which the apparent shape of an object remains constant despite changes in the shape of the retinal image

Size Constancy
Size constancy is the stability of perceived size despite changes in objective distance and retinal image size.

Tessellation
A tessellation is a tiling (or repeated design) which can be extended infinitely in any direction.

Vestibular System
The vestibular system monitors the body's movement and orientation in space and is the principle organ of balance and is located in the middle ear.

Visual Angle
Visual angle is a measure of image size on the retina, corresponding to the number of degrees the image subtends from its extremes to the focal point of the eye

Visual Field
The visual field is comprised of all the stimuli you can see, even those a few degrees away from the center of your focus.

Further Reading

Block, J. Richard and Yuker, H., *Can You Believe Your Eyes?*
Gardner Press, Inc., 1989

Cobb, Vicki, *How to Really Fool Yourself: Illusions for all Your Senses*,
John Wiley and Sons, Inc., 1999

*Coren, Stanley and Girgus, J. S., *Seeing is Deceiving: The
Psychology of Visual Illusions*, Erlbaum Press, 1978

Ernst, Bruno, *The Eye Beguiled: Optical Illusions*,
Benedikt Taschen, 1992

*Frisby, John, *Seeing: Illusion, Brain and Mind*,
Oxford University Press, 1980

Goldstein, E. Bruce, *Sensation and Perception: Fourth edition*,
Wadsworth, 1997

Gregory, Richard, *Eye and Brain: Fifth Edition*,
Princeton University Press, 1997

Gregory, Richard and Gombrich, E. H., *Illusion in Nature and Art*,
Gerald Duckworth, 1980

Hoffman, Donald, *Visual Intelligence: How We Create What We See*,
W. W. Norton & Company, 1998

*Palmer, Stephen, *Vision Science: Photons to Phenomenology*,
The MIT Press, 1999

*Robinson, J. O., *The Psychology of Visual Illusion*,
Dover Publications, 1998

Rock, Irvin, *Perception*, Scientific American Library, 1984

Rodgers, Nigel, *Incredible Optical Illusions*, Barnes and Noble, 1998

Shepard, Roger, *Mind Sights*, W. H. Freeman and Company, 1990

*Spillman, Lothar and John Werner, *Visual Perception: The
Neurophysiological Foundations*, Academic Press, 1990

*Advanced reading

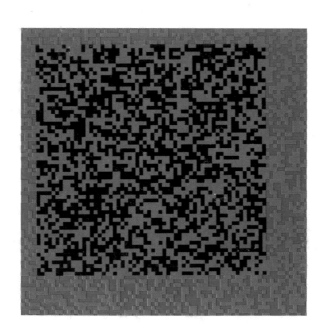